er · Geppert Co.

ews Sanford. Copyright © 1938, 1966.   The Ronald Press Company, New York.

Sport in Classic Times

FOUR-IN-HAND.

Pelops and Hippodamia.

From an Attic vase c. 400 B.C.

Frontispiece.

SPORT IN CLASSIC TIMES

by

A. J. Butler, D.Litt.

Fellow of Brasenose College, Oxford
Fellow of Eton College

FOREWORD BY RODERICK HAIG-BROWN

William Kaufmann, Inc.
Los Altos, California

Artemis was goddess of hunting and fishing in parts of
ancient Greece. The jacket illustration of Artemis with fish,
birds, animals and other symbols is taken from *Ephemeris
Archelogigue*. Artemis is also identified with Diana,
goddess of hunting, chastity and the moon in
Roman mythology.

Library of Congress Cataloging in Publication Data

Butler, Alfred Joshua, 1850-1936.
  Sport in classic times.

  Reprint of the 1930 ed. published by E. Benn, London
  Bibliography: p.
  1. Hunting--Greece--History. 2. Hunting--Rome--
History. 3. Fishing--Greece--History. 4. Fishing--
Rome--History. 5. Classical antiquities. I. Title.
SK203.B87 1974   799'.0938   74-12191
ISBN 0-913232-13-0

FOREWORD

In the Halls of the Heroes there have always been great sportsmen, great hunters, great catchers of fish, men like gods in the tales of their successors. In their own time, no doubt, they were mere mortals, subject like other men to rain and cold and weariness and failure. Some may not even have been highly regarded by their peers until the tale tellers gathered up the incidents of remembered greatness and told them in the red light of the fires on the long evenings.

The origins of sport may well have been in this. Living, mortal men, hearing the tales, would set out later to test themselves against the heroes. For any true and fair test there must be standards of a sort, or heroes can be matched only in endless argument and speculation. Once there are standards, pure pragmatism ends and sport begins. The objective is no longer simply to bring home food, but to demonstrate achievement as well.

In the hero there is always some subtle refinement of skill and instinct that goes beyond anything readily explained. The man of hounds will remember his hero's supernatural knowledge of country, his anticipation of his quarry's line of flight, his ability to lift hounds at check unerringly on to the true scent. The game hunter remembers the mysterious, infallible woodcraft of his models, their superb marksmanship and their superhuman endurance in the face of storm and distance. The angler recalls legendary feats of streamcraft, full creels under conditions that were barren for others, subtle re-finements of method. Such things are the lively seeds of tradition and sport is the offspring of tradition. It becomes an acceptance of restraints that enhance pleasure and embellish achievement even as they limit mere efficiency.

Mankind loves to search into the origins of its arts, customs and behavior, and wisely so because the exercise has many rewards, pragmatic as well as aesthetic. On the North American continent today hunting and fishing, the two great field sports, count their adherents by millions. There is at least one fishing rod or "fish-pole" in practically every household and most of these see use at some time in every year. There are certainly far too many guns in far too many households, variously unused, misused or abused. But there is also a good proportion of sporting weapons that are used for sporting purposes. There are bows and arrows also, in increasing numbers, and two instruments unknown to the Ancients, the camera and the field glass, both capable of yielding most intense satisfactions to wildlife enthusiasts. In terms of challenge to hunting skills, sound nerves and steady thinking the camera may well be the sportsman's ultimate weapon, on the land and under the water.

This immensity of popular interest in the outdoors, wildlife and the field sports is unprecedented and makes re-publication of Dr. Butler's scholarly and charming SPORT IN CLASSIC TIMES particularly useful and appropriate. We are, of course, already asking ourselves what are the ecological, sociological and economic implications of enthusiasm for field sports—Plato and others seem to have asked hard questions too—but the truly interesting questions are more spiritual and more deeply philosophic than these. What are our traditions and sanctions? How deeply is love of the wild a part of man?

How important is it to the health and well-being of modern man?

I believe without hesitation that the cave painters of Lascaux were lovers of wildlife and of the beauty of wildlife; I believe, too, that they were lovers of hunting and of the intensity of experience it can afford. They have left no written record, but all this is in the quality and emotional values of the paintings. Undoubtedly they were hunters of food in a truly primitive sense of necessity; but there was much more to it than that.

The cave painters lived and hunted thousands of years before the Greeks and Romans, and the Greeks and Romans knew nothing of them directly. Yet it seems not altogether unlikely that some dim trace of verbal tradition carried through the millenia to men like Xenophon, Oppian and Arrian and contributed to their keen concern for the craft and mystique of hunting. Dr. Butler shows very clearly the love and respect these writers had for horse and hound and quarry, for the subtleties of the chase, the intricacies of gear and the unwritten rules that make the difference between sport and slaughter.

Dr. Butler's book is worth any modern sportsman's while for its introduction to Arrian alone. Arrian was a sportsman in the full modern sense of the word, as well as a woodsman and a human being of a very high order. All these qualities are revealed in Dr. Butler's quotation on page 30, and the release of the hunted hare compares quite closely to the "catch and release" code of so many modern fly fishermen.

Greek and Roman hunting seems to have involved hounds almost invariably and horses often enough. Any modern hunter of foxes, rabbits, raccoons, opossums or cougars will recognise the keen discussion of the qualities and conformation of hounds. Larger animals were brought to bay, smaller ones, such as hares, were driven into nets (unsporting) or simply run down, much as hares and foxes are today. There is no mention of animals being driven to tree, which is surprising in view of the references to "pards, wild cats and panthers." Perhaps these animals, like the North American bobcat, had the strength and endurance to keep ahead of hounds and hunters through long hours of chase. At all events, they seem not to have been considered desirable quarry. Arrian's account of a favorite hunting dog again stands out. Strains and breeds—Molossian, Arcanian, Agassaean (the British dog of war) are compared and discussed much as modern hunters examine the qualities of foxhound, bloodhound, blue tick and redbone and their crosses. The spirit and enthusiasm have changed little in two thousand years.

Comparisons suggest themselves all through the book. Oppian's confused and exciting account of a whale hunt contrasts with the much bolder and more efficient whale hunting of the Nootka and Makah Indians of the Pacific Coast of North America, which may well have been contemporary. The shore nets for wildfowl bring to mind similar nets noticed on the northern end of the Olympic Peninsula by Captain George Vancouver in 1792. Dr. Butler points out that the famous feat of marksmanship, in which Arthur Philipson, in Walter Scott's "Ann of Geierstein," shot three arrows in rapid succession with supreme and dramatic precision is borrowed from Vergil, who in turn borrowed it from Homer. The famous Athapascan Indian, Long Ba'tiste, guide, hunter and friend of miners in the British Columbia gold rush and later hunting guide to Judge Matthew Baillie Begbie, performed a similar feat just over a hundred years ago. The occasion was a gathering of Indian tribes and miners at Lac La Hache. Long Ba'tiste first took on all comers in wrestling and footraces and tests of strength. Then, with his bow, he outshot the miners' long rifles at distant marks and concluded the exercise by shooting two arrows through a hat thrown in the air before it could reach the ground. It seems unlikely that the miners who recorded the event would have known Vergil or Homer's stories, but they may well have read Scott and so perpetuated a great tradition.

Horsehair lines and leaders were preferred by the Ancients for some kinds of fishing—hairs from the tail of a white stallion preferred, as they were in Dame Juliana's "Treatyse of Fysshynge With An Angle," first published in England thirteen centuries later (1496), and by most writers after her up to the end of the last century. My friend Tom Brayshaw, the artist and a great fisherman on any water in any company, learned to fly fish in the 1890's with a tapered horsehair line and horsehair leaders. No doubt horsehair was used long before Ælian's time around 100 A.D. so it had a great run before silk line and silk-worm gut came to replace it late in the 19th century. Today you would search a long way to find a fly fisherman using anything but a plastic line and nylon leaders. We fishermen have become a sadly restless bunch, though I suppose it could be said that we now need spend less time looking after our gear and so have more for contemplation. I wonder if we use it for honest contemplation or simply for the mental exercise that yields a proliferation of new gadgets?

A good part of the charm of field sports—and Dr. Butler makes the distinction between these and athletic sports very clearly—is in their relaxed ways: the absence of competition, the peace of woods and streams and wilderness, the silent movement, the close observation of wildlife, the sensitivity to all things that affect wild-life, from wind and weather to trees and shrubs and plants. The Ancients were well aware of these charms and challenges. Their knowledge may have been simpler than ours, as their weapons and gear were certainly less sophisticated. But they were following tradition and developing tradition for us. They were hunting not only their quarry, but knowledge and understanding and keener pleasure.

To this end they set up and refined their unwritten rules: the hare should be run down in the open by honest hound work, not trapped by nets; poisoning fish was an unworthy act, as were other cruel and excessively efficient means of taking them; the imitation of the horsetail fly no doubt was efficient, but there was also a special charm and excitement in its use, recognised and built upon by other fly fishermen to this day.

The Ancients knew the sense of belonging in nature that comes to man through woodcraft and streamcraft, and sought always to enhance it by subtle and perceptive approaches. They tested their endurance and wearied themselves and rested. They fought with dense brush, swamps and mountain slopes even as we do today. They endured rain and cold and rough water, battled storms and suffered heat. They knew their quarry and never tired of learning more about its ways. It is good to feel fellowship over the centuries with Xenophon, Oppian, Ælian, Arrian and the others, even with the stern considerations of Plato, most certainly with the early exactitudes and fancies of Aristotle. Dr. Butler's book has its place in the literature of sport and it is satisfying to know that it will once again be readily available.

Roderick Haig-Brown

CAMPBELL RIVER
BRITISH COLUMBIA
JANUARY 1975

PREFACE

A THOUSAND books have been written on the art, and ten thousand on the language, literature, life, and history of the Greeks and Romans; yet even in these days of commerce-worship and machine-rule the interest in such studies has deepened, if not widened, and the knowledge grows clearer that without its classical background modern culture would be lacking in the best elements of its composition and colour. Quite apart from many recent enlargements of the field of research, there has been a quickening of the desire to look more closely into and to realise more fully the actual life of the peoples of antiquity, both from curiosity and from hope of understanding their spirit and genius.

Yet with all this awakening interest, and with all the making of books, some of which bring much weariness of the flesh to reader as well as to writer, not one book has been written on the field sports of the Greeks and Romans. A real contribution to the study of one branch of the subject has been made by Mr. Radcliffe in his admirable Fishing from the Earliest Times; and Professor Mair, in the Loeb edition of Oppian, has produced a work of distinguished research: to both volumes I wish to acknowledge my debt. But this essay has a much wider compass and design, inasmuch as it endeavours to open out for the English reader a whole province of the classical world which has been left almost entirely unsurveyed.

The love of sport is a fact in human nature which no amount of austere talk or kindly sentiment can ever banish; and the place of sport in classical life and thought cannot be a matter of great indifference— even to classical pedants. That Plato had studied all the details of sport in his philosophy, and that Xenophon was the greatest sportsman of his age, may or may not be known; but few can realise how near in spirit and in working were many of the forms of ancient sport to those of today, or how amusingly varied were the crafts of the sportsman and his mysteries. There is matter here which, it is hoped, may interest some of those who have forgotten or ill understood their classics, as they hark to the music of hounds or view them racing on a burning scent; as they hear the boar crashing through the brake amid the flash of spears and the shouts of men, or as they watch the calm excitement of the angler casting his fly on a trout stream or playing a goodly fish. Scenes like these may even freshen the schoolboy's imagination and enable him to think of Greeks and Romans not as phantoms or dullards who moved long ago in a dim world of shadows, but as men who lived in sunshine, who loved field and mountain and river, and who were masters of every form of sport, as they were masters of every form of art and literature.

TABLE OF CONTENTS

vii

LIST OF ILLUSTRATIONS

ix

LIST OF CLASSICAL AUTHORITIES
APPROXIMATELY DATED

The date is to be understood as *flor. circa.*

AElian		
Naturalis Historia ⎫		
Varia Historia ⎭	130	A.D.
AEschylus . .	480	B.C.
Alciphron . .	?200	A.D.
Anthologia Palatina		v.d.
Aristophanes . .	430	B.C.
Aristotle . .	340	B.C.
Arrian . .	100	A.D.
Athenaeus . .	230	A.D.
Aulus Gellius .	150	A.D.
Ausonius . .	350	A.D.
Bion . .	280	B.C.
Caesar . .	50	B.C.
Cicero . .	60	B.C.
Claudian . .	450	A.D.
Dionysius Periegetes .	?200	A.D.
Euripides .	440	B.C.
Grattius or *Gratius* .	10	B C.
Herodotus . .	450	B.C.
Hesiod . .	?800	B.C.
Homer . .	850	B.C.
Horace . .	30	B.C.
Ion . .	450	B.C.
Ixeutica (see *Dionysius*)		

Juvenal . . .	80	A.D.
Lucan . . .	50	A.D.
Lucian . . .	160	A.D.
Martial . . .	80	A.D.
Nemesianus . .	260	A.D.
Oppian . .	180	A.D.
Ovid . . .	20	B.C.
Pausanias . .	180	A.D.
Pindar . . .	490	B.C.
Plato . . .	390	B.C.
Pliny the Elder .	50	A.D.
Pliny the Younger .	100	A.D.
Plutarch . .	80	A.D.
Pollux . . .	180	A.D.
Sallust . . .	60	B.C.
Seneca . . .	10	B.C.
Silius Italicus .	80	A.D.
Strabo . . .	20	B.C.
Tacitus . .	100	A.D.
Valerius Flaccus .	70	A.D.
Varro . . .	50	B.C.
Vegetius . .	30	A.D.
Vergil . . .	40	B.C.
Xenophon . .	400	B.C.

All translations and paraphrases, including verses from the Greek Anthology, are the Author's own work.

SPORT IN CLASSIC TIMES

CHAPTER I

FORMS OF SPORT

Hunting—Fishing—Fowling.

ALL who have ever known the joy of hunting or fishing or fowling know that each form of sport has its doughty champions, ready and willing to drive a lance through the breast of any devotee of another form who dare enter the lists against them. Ready and willing, no doubt, but quite powerless to overthrow their rivals: the lance misses its mark, glides aside, or splinters at a touch, and the rivals quit the field none the worse for the encounter, but each more firmly convinced that the charms of his own particular mistress are incomparable.

In modern literature records of such strife are familiar enough, the most familiar being that in the Compleat Angler, where the dialogue ambles along rather like a sermon in which personal predilection, sacred authority, and queer logic are amusingly or amazingly blended. But there is nothing of this kind to be found in the earliest classical writers. Homer sings of the glories of the chase, and the same thought runs woven in clear colours through the fabric of Greek mythology; whereas fishing and fowling had to pass through a long period of service as mere utilities before they could win admission to the rank of sports. Plato,[1] after speaking of Sophists as " troublesome creatures, very hard to capture," gives a rough analysis of fishing and hunting. But it is not till we come to

[1] Soph. 219.

Oppian, several centuries later, that the three
forms of sport are definitely contrasted, something
in the manner of Izaak Walton, in respect of their
different amenities. Even Walton, however, does
not sever the pleasure of sport from its usefulness
as a means of providing food; as witness the quaint
remark of Auceps on fowling, that birds " feed man
with their choice bodies and refresh him with their
heavenly voices "—a remark which might almost suggest a dish of nightingales. On the question of the
balance between the ideas of pleasure and profit in
the Greek and Roman conception of sport there is
some disagreement, which arises mainly from a
failure on the part of writers who are no sportsmen
to understand that the two elements are and always
were inseparable.

What of modern hunting? it will be said.
Hunting today means fox-hunting in the broad
use of the term, and there of course no question
of providing food arises. But the profit of the sport
is health and hardiness and boldness and training
in quick judgment and decision, all of which come
with enjoyment of the chase. Moreover, it must
be remembered that fox-hunting is a form of sport
hardly known as a pastime to the ancients and
unknown even in England two centuries ago. We
are not concerned, therefore, with a very modern
form of sport which is no purveyor of food, though
it will be very easy to establish the fact that in
classic times the need for finding food, which in the
early ages of man had been the great incentive to
the chase, and which still remained a strong motive,
was often lost in the sheer enjoyment of matching
and overcoming the strength and swiftness and cunning of the quarry—in other words, was lost in the
love of sport.

Oppian wrote somewhere about A.D. 180, and we
must, for our present purpose, avoid all question

of his single or dual personality.[1] His poems represent the three main divisions of animal life, birds, beasts, and fishes—as corresponding with three several forms of pursuit or hunting, as it must be called for want of a better generic name—and they find their scope in air and on land and on sea; in fowling, hunting proper, and fishing; and all he calls delightful. Yet on comparison the stakes are very unequal for fowler, hunter, and fisherman. All, no doubt, have a set task; but pleasure alone attends the pursuit of fowler and angler, without any stain of blood. The angler sits on a rock by the sea at his ease, and his line with baited hooks hangs from a bending rod. He has only to feel the touch of a fish, then strikes home, and, full of excitement, flings him high out of the water on to the land. The same joy in his sport has the fowler, who carries no sword or spear or weapon of war, but goes off to the forest with his falcon, or his net and cords, or bird-lime, and jointed rods which he lengthens by imperceptible stages, stealing upon his prey. But the hunter has to follow and fight with wild beasts of the mountain at peril of life and limb; and how can this pursuit be thrown into a balance against the gentle craft of angling or fowling? As well set an eagle against a lion, a sea-urchin against a rhinoceros, a gull against an ibex. The hunter deals death to the wolf, while the fisherman spears a tunny, and the bird-man catches doves: the hunter chases bear or wild boar or tiger, while the angler pulls sea-bream or mullet out of the water, and the fowler catches nightingales.

Such, roughly, is Oppian's comparison of the merit of the three sports, and it rests on an estimate of the amount of danger attending them severally. On this score he has no difficulty in awarding pre-eminence to hunting, which requires youth and

[1] See Prof. Mair's Oppian, p. xxii (Loeb Classics).

dash and courage and hardihood, while he implies
that angling and fowling are sheltered amusements,
depending largely on tricks of skill with the weapons
of the craft, which are wielded at comfortable leisure.
It will be seen when we come to his Treatise on
Fishing, that he has to revise this judgement—almost
to reverse it—pointing out that the perils of storm
and wreck at sea are more formidable than any
perils of the land.   But hunting, as it is the oldest
and the most familiar form of sport in classic literature, is entitled to be considered first on its own
merits and apart from any comparison.

CHAPTER II

ON HUNTING AND ITS ADVANTAGES

Homer—Orion—Artemis—Xenophon—Ladies at the Chase—
Plato's Views—Hunting and War.

IT is perhaps curious that in the Old Testament there is no mention of horse or hound for use in the chase; nor is there any hint that Nimrod, the mighty hunter, depended upon anything but his own bow and spear and speed. On the other hand, Homer, whose date may be fixed with reasonable certainty to the middle of the ninth century B.C., always associates hounds with the hunter. Thus, in the story of Meleager and the boar, he tells of him as

πολλέων ἐκ πολίων θηρήτορας ἄνδρας ἀγείρων
καὶ κύνας.[1]

So when Odysseus, returning home from his long wandering, sees the old retainer Eumaeus and the old dog Argos,[2] he enquires if Argos was ever of use in the field, as he must have been good-looking, or was he a mere house-dog, trencher-fed?[3] Eumaeus praises his whilom strength and speed; his nose was as keen as his pace was swift, and not a beast of the forest could escape him. In the same passage one reads of wild goats and deer as followed by young

---

[1] Il. IX. 538.   [2] Od. XVII. 295 and 316.
[3] The Greek expression, more literally *table-hound*, corresponds verbally to this term as defined by Mr. Jorrocks in Handley Cross. But the meaning differs. A trencher-fed hound in modern parlance is one put out to walk at farm or cottage, away from kennels: with Homer it means a house-dog as opposed to a sporting dog.

MELEAGER AND THE BOAR.
From a Pompeian painting.

Notice the two spears and the sun-hats.

huntsmen—young, for the chase was no child's play;
and Homer, elsewhere describing the isle of the
Cyclops, brings out well the requirement of hardihood—

οὔτε μιν εἰσοιχνεῦσι κυνηγέται, οἵ τε καθ' ὕλην
ἄλγεα πάσχουσιν.[1]

Elsewhere[2] a boar-hunt is described more closely
when a hunting party—clearly for sport—is arranged, and the sons of Autolycus take Odysseus
with them to the wooded heights and the wind-
swept hollows of Mount Parnassus. The hounds
in front, and Odysseus close behind carrying a
long spear, they came at last to a dense covert in
the forest so thick that neither sun nor wind could
pierce through it, and here a huge boar harboured.
He heard the voices of men and the patter of hounds
in the thicket, and stood up with mane bristling
and eyes flashing fire. Odysseus cast his spear and
missed, whereupon the boar charged and grazed
his thigh, but with another spear Odysseus thrust
home and killed him.

The delight and the triumph of the chase, as well
as its danger, are clearly marked in this little story.
One may also note that in Homer's time, as always,
the big-game hunter carried two spears, one for
throwing and the other for use at close quarters,[3]
and that, whereas in after days the hunter aimed not
so much at direct encounter as at driving the quarry
towards a netted enclosure, there is no mention
whatever in Homer of nets for use in the chase.

One or two more incidents from Homer may be
given. Scamandrius, whom he calls (like Nimrod)
a mighty hunter, had been trained by Artemis

---

[1] Od. IX. 120.   [2] Od. XIX. 429 *seq.*

[3] This expression is actually used by Xenophon, Cyr. I. 2. 9:
ὥστε τὸ μὲν ἀφεῖναι, τῷ δὲ ἂν δέῃ ἐκ χειρὸς χρῆσθαι. Two spears
are also mentioned in other lines of Homer, in Vergil, and elsewhere, and are shown generally on vases and in paintings.

herself to bring down every kind of wild beast bred
in the mountain forests, and was renowned for his
long-distance shooting, but was slain by Menelaus.[1]
This same Artemis is called πότνια θηρῶν,[2] Queen
of the Chase, and Heré taunts her with the remark
that " It is wiser to go killing wild deer on the
mountains than to do battle against your betters."
Once more, when Odysseus in the world of the
dead meets the gigantic Orion, he finds him

θῆρας ὁμοῦ εἰλεῦντα κατ᾽ ἀσφόδελον λειμῶνα
τοὺς αὐτὸς κατέπεφνεν ἐν οἰοπόλοισιν ὄρεσσιν[3]

chasing over the asphodel meadow the wild beasts
he had slain in life on the lonely uplands: and in
Orion's love of field sports, as his strongest passion,
surviving beyond the grave, one may trace the same
belief as that of the Red Indian in happy hunting-
grounds after death, or that of the Muslim in a
houri-peopled paradise, or that of many serious
philosophers and theologians today, who hold that
man's soul must carry into the life beyond those
passions and those thoughts which shaped and domin-
ated his life here on earth, and hardened into habit
of mind.

In Homer for the most part the hunting was for
the larger game. Mention is made of a couple of
well-trained hounds pursuing fawn or hare.[4] On
the shield of Achilles is wrought a hunt of two
lions which were raiding cattle;[5] while in another
passage wild goats, deer, and hares, are named as
objects of the chase.[6] In fact the truth must be
set clear that the poet only gives here and there

---

[1] Il. V. 49.
[2] Il. XXI. 480, a passage which Oppian may have had in mind
when he calls Artemis πότνα θεά, παγκοίρανε θήρης, Sovran Queen
of the Chase.
[3] Od. XI. 572. It may be noted that Orion carried a powerful
mace of metal.
[4] Il. X. 360.　　　　[5] Il. XVIII. 577.　　　　[6] Od. XVII. 295.

glimpses of that vast tradition of sport which was highly developed a thousand years before him. Hesiod, in the Shield of Heracles—if it was written by Hesiod—speaks of hare-hunting in terms apparently borrowed from Homer:

τοὶ δ᾽ ὠκύποδας λαγὸς ᾕρεῦν
ἄνδρες θηρευταὶ καὶ χαρχαρόδοντε κύνε πρό,[1]

i.e., hunters, each man with his couple of hounds, were shown capturing fleet-footed hares; and this was one of the scenes embossed upon the shield. Some lines lower comes[2] a description of a wild boar, gnashing and foaming, with eyes aflame,

BOAR AND STAGS.
From a Pompeian painting.

against a ring of hunters in a mountain forest; but this, too, looks like a reminiscence of Homer: and there are other reasons for thinking that the poem may belong to a later date than Hesiod. However that may be, as more and more waste land was brought into tillage and all the plains were planted with grain or green crops, the country became far more likely for hares, while the beasts of the forest had their range shortened and their mountain lairs were thrown more open to their enemies. The hare was thus provided with better cover and clearer runs, with a field of less danger from some of her

[1] Shield of Heracles, I 303.   [2] Id. I 386.

foes; and, as the hare bred more freely, hare-hunting became so popular a pastime that in later chronicles of sport it takes almost the highest place.

So when Xenophon, the great general and leader of the Ten Thousand, writes of hunting, he is generally thinking of hare-hunting, though his Treatise on Hunting contains chapters on the chase of the stag, wild-boar, lion, pard, and bear. Xenophon was born about 444 B.C., and his experience in war taught him the great practical value of that hard riding and hunting which he loved to practise on his country estate in Elis. The opening words of his Treatise run: " Game and hounds are devised of the gods—Apollo and Artemis to wit"; and he cites many stories of heroes and warriors in legend or history, whose prowess arose from training in the field and shone in deeds which rendered them saviours of Hellas. So he adds: " I counsel young men not to look down on hunting or other forms of training which fit them for war and for divers situations where quick thought and word and action are required." In a later chapter[1] this theme is worked out more fully, and the writer gives in more detail the lessons learnt from his own generalship.

Love of the chase, he says, brings health of body, keenness of sight and hearing; it prolongs youth; but above all it is good training for war. Men used to hunting, when marching under arms through difficult country, will not turn faint or slacken, but will be braced against hardships, since it was only by dint of hardship that they were trained to capture their quarry. In an advance against the enemy they will show at once the spirit of attack and the spirit of discipline—both qualities required in the chase. If set in the front line of battle, they will

---

[1] Ch. XII. I commend to all interested Mr. Marchant's edition with English translation in the Loeb Classics.

not quit their ranks, but will act with the courage
they have acquired in the hunting-field. They will
pursue, when the foe is turned, in good order and
security over any kind of ground; while if they
meet with a reverse, they can retreat without danger
and can help their comrades through moor or forest
or mountain gorge. In fact the " eye for country "
which they developed in hunting will serve them in
good stead in victory or defeat, and it has often
happened that a handful of troops so trained with
discipline and resource have faced about against a
mass of pursuers entangled in rough bush or broken
ground, and have driven them off with heavy loss.
In this Xenophon is surely recalling incidents in
the Retreat of the Ten Thousand.[1]

But apart from all military advantage, great is the
moral value of athletic and field sports, which seem
to have been denounced by those sophists or sham
philosophers who darkened counsel against right
and reason, and on whom his argument falls heavily.
It may be noted that Lycurgus ordained at Sparta
that both sexes alike should engage in athletic
exercises, and women were to have their own
competitions of strength and speed.[2] Those who
rebuke young fellows for their love of hunting
forget all the service they render to the State and
the family. Moreover, all the men who have been
devoted to the chase have been good characters,
and so have those women to whom Artemis has
given the like happiness, such as Atalanta and
Procris.

Can this be taken to mean that in Xenophon's
day women were sometimes seen in the field ?

---

[1] Athenaeus, who was a little after Oppian, agrees with Xenophon:
" Young fellows," he says, " go out hunting for practice against
the perils of war, and follow every form of the chase which renders
them stronger and healthier." Deip. I. 24c.

[2] See Xen. Pol. 1. Modern physiologists seem on the whole to
approve such training for women

Vergil makes Dido ride out to the chase, wearing
gorgeous apparel more suitable for the drawing-
room of her palace, though she carried a quiver of
gold by her side.   In art and in legend the Amazon
is a familiar figure as huntress and warrior, and the
first who ever shot arrows at her quarry, the boar,
is said to have been the maiden huntress Atalanta.[1]

So Daphne was renowned for hunting with her
maidens, and when Leucippus fell in love with her,
and knew her aversion to men, he let his hair grow,
plaited it, and donned a woman's robe, so that as
the daughter of a prince he could ask leave to join
her in the chase.   By his address, and above all by
his knowledge of the whole art of hunting, he became
her welcome companion, until his sex was discovered
and he perished by the spears which Daphne and
her maidens flung upon him.[2]

But there is an instance which comes home with
greater force in Euripides.   He depicts Phaedra as
passionately devoted (like her husband, Theseus) to
the chase.   Striving in agony to escape from her
unholy love, "Take me to the mountain side," she
cries: "away to the pine forest where the hounds
that slay are running and pressing hard upon the
dappled deer.   Oh Heaven! how I long to be
hallooing to my hounds, and hurling the lance from
the level of my golden locks, as I poise the hunting-
spear on my arm."   It is fairly clear that she must
be thought of as mounted and holding the hunting-
spear in her bridle hand; at any rate that she was no
less accomplished as horsewoman than as huntress
is shown by other lines in the same chorus, which
may be rendered thus in verse:

[1] Oppian, Cyn. II. 26.

Σχοινῆος πρώτη δὲ κλυτὴ θυγάτηρ Ἀταλάντη
Θηρσὶ φόνον πτερόεντα συήβολος εὕρετο κούρη.

[2] Pausanias, VIII. 20.

Artemis, queen of the ocean main,
    Queen of the racing-grounds
    Where the ringing hoof resounds,
O set me within thine empire's bounds
    With fierce wild colts to break and rein.[1]

The link between Artemis as queen of the sea and
as queen of racing in this passage is that the best
of all courses to the Greeks—that for the Isthmian
games—was a long stretch of hard level sand on the
seashore, as is very clearly shown by another passage
in the same play, where the thoughts of hunting in
wooded hills and racing along a silvery beach are
closely linked together.[2]   But while Phaedra is thus
depicted as a fearless and enthusiastic lover of
horses and hounds, Euripides, with all his hatred of
women, amid all the storms of reproach that are
launched at Phaedra's unhappy head, never betrays
the slightest hint that her sportsmanship could be
regarded as unfeminine.   Such a taunt, however, he
never would have spared if the idea of ladies taking
part in the chase had been either unfamiliar to, or
unpopular with, the Athenians of his day.

This is a fair inference; but more direct evidence
of the same tenour is furnished by a fresco, discovered early this century at Tiryns, which represents two ladies in a chariot watching hounds as
they run into a wild boar.[3]   These hounds, it may
be noted, are all of one breed, with the same marking
or mottling, and all wear collars, showing that they

---

[1] The two passages are from the Hippolytus, 215-222 and
228-231.   A few lines earlier Phaedra had cried: "O for a cooling
draft from some sparkling rill !   O for the poplar shade and long
waving meadow grass, where I might lay me down and take my
rest:" and the change of mood from rest, first to the joyous activity
of the chase, and then to the mad excitement of breaking young
horses, is most dramatic.

[2] Hippol. 1126-1134.

[3] Tiryns, by G. Rodenwaldt (Athens, 1912), II. 96 *seq.* and
pls. 12 *seq.*

have been slipped from the leash at the right
moment, as required by the rules of the hunt.

There is, then, some ground for thinking that
ladies in Greece in classic times were given to hunting, and we know that those of romantic legend who
hunted were mostly very virtuous, and so con-
formed to Xenophon's canon that virtue adorns all
followers of the hounds—a fact which doubtless is
amply confirmed by the records of the shires in
England. Dido of Carthage was no doubt, like
Phaedra, an exception in her time: possibly there
may be other exceptions today.

Plato, in his Book of Laws, has some remarks
on various forms of sport, addressed to young men
and worth quoting: " I hope no yearning, no passion,
for sea-fishing or angling will ever get hold of you,
nor any pursuit of water-animals, nor the idle
sport of setting day and night weels.[1]   The beguiling
pastime of fowling must be avoided as hardly worthy
of a gentleman.   There remains only for our sportsmen the hunting of four-footed creatures, and the
chase of them at night-time when they are asleep is
an idle business, and far from commendable; so is
the use of nets and snares, which involves intervals
of resting, and is far apart from that spirit of stark
endeavour required to conquer the ruthless strength
of your quarry.   Alone, and surpassing all, stands
the pursuit of wild animals with horse and hound by
the hunter in person.   By racing, fighting, slinging
and chasing, in personal encounter, those prevail
who have at heart the ideal of manhood.   These
hunters are devoted to good," he continues, " and

[1] Legg. VII. *sub fin.* I cannot agree with Jowett's rendering
here. He makes it appear that Plato cautioned his hearers not to
allow the passion of angling to take possession of them " either when
they are awake or when they are asleep," whereas the waking
and sleeping clearly refer to the weels, which work day and
night without any effort on the part of the fisherman. The fact
that this kind of sport needs no personal exertion is that which
condemns it in Plato's judgment.

the law for them shall run: ' Let no man interfere with them, wherever they choose to hunt.' "

This teaching of Plato persisted with extraordinary force to a late date. Thus Vegetius, who wrote on the Art of War about the year A.D. 400, says: " I hold that anglers and fowlers must not be allowed anywhere near a training-camp, but hunters of stags and wild boars will be welcome recruits."[1]

So much for Plato: but the belief in hunting as training for war is a living belief and not a mere relic of antiquity. During his wars in France Edward III kept sixty couples of stag-hounds and sixty couples of harriers, mainly, no doubt, as diversion for his officers and men, but the fact is proof that his armies were trained to sport. Wellington kept a pack of foxhounds in the Peninsula; and readers of Marbot's Memoirs will remember his naive astonishment at the ease and speed with which our cavalry officers were accustomed to clear all obstacles when scouting, to appear in impossible places, and to vanish, their purpose accomplished. Nor can one forget how much of their fine performance in the Great War and before it that splendid force, the English Yeomanry, owed to their love of horn and hounds.

And what of today? The idea remains; but changes in the temper and the pursuits of army cadets, changes in the shattered and half-mended structure of society, suggest to a soldier of the old school the question, " Will our officers, in days to come, still be able to lead without hunting to develop their ' eye for a country,' or polo to train them in the habit of quick decision ?"[2]

Mr. Jorrocks might still say that hunting is the sport of kings, but hardly that it is the image of war.

[1] De Re Militari, Cap. VII.
[2] " Saddle and Steel," by Lord Dunalley, pref.

CHAPTER III

THE HUNTER AS SPORTSMAN, AND HIS EQUIPMENT

Keen Sense of Sport—Xenophon and Arrian—True Sportsmanship—Hare Hunting—Qualities and Weapons Required—
Spear, Knife, Bow.

THE question has been raised how far hunting
was regarded in classic times as a sport, and
how far as a business. Something has already been
said upon this question in an earlier chapter; but
all doubt about a purely sporting spirit in the chase
can be swept aside in a few words. Apart from
deductions from Homer and from folklore before
him, Xenophon alone would be decisive. " Our
ancestors," he writes, " well knew that the sheer
pleasure of the chase brings the greatest advantage
to young hunters;"[1] and again he uses a very strong
expression—" to be in love with hunting."[2] He
has also a definite word for " sportsman," φιλοκυνη-
γέτης; and how closely his conception of the term
corresponds with that of today is shown by his
remark that a true sportsman leaves young leverets
alone and does not attempt to kill them. And
what could be clearer than words like these ? Speaking of the hare doubling and often baffling hounds,
he says: " So charming is the sight, that to view the
questing for the hare, the find, the coursing, and the
kill, would make anyone forget the dearest love of
his heart."

Arrian of Nicomedia, who wrote at a much later

[1] τῶν νεωτέρων ἡ ἡδονὴ μόνη αὐτὴ πλεῖστα ἀγαθὰ παρασκευάζει.
[2] ἐρᾶν κυνηγεσιῶν denotes passionate love.

28

date,[1] adds a further touch of refinement to the idea
of sport, when, speaking of the Celts of Western
France, he distinguishes those among them who
hunt for a livelihood, using nets, and those who
hunt without nets " for the sheer beauty of the
chase "—[2] words which designedly, I think, if only
half seriously, recall something of the Platonic ideal
of the highest good, while they touch that sense of
mystery and delight in nature, which so often comes
home to those who follow field sports with a mind
open to the strange yet familiar magic of woodland
and wold and river. Some thought of the kind
runs through a fine passage in Oppian, a century
later. Speaking of Orion and other heroic figures,
" These," he says, " of old were the mighty captains
of the chase: but many in after times were en-
thralled by the stirring passion, and no man once
taken captive by love of the charms of hunting
can ever forsake it again of free will—so overpowering are the bonds that hold him." Then he gives
a romantic picture of a day in the field. " Think
how sweet is slumber upon the wild flowers in
springtime: how pleasant to lie on the floor of a
cave in summer heat: what charm there is in a meal
on the mountain side: how delightful to pluck
with one's own hand in passing the mellow fruits
of autumn: and the cool crystal stream welling out
from some rocky recess—what a drink for the
thirsty does it give and a bathe for weary limbs.
Herdsmen too, tending their flocks among the wood-
lands, give welcome with baskets of cheering gifts."[3]

Here the simple love of life in the open and the
joy of the countryside are graven on the poet's
mind, on which no trace is drawn of pleasure in
mere killing or capturing the prey. It would be
idle to deny that this pleasure counted for much in

---

[1] About 100 A.D.   [2] αὐτοῦ τοῦ ἐν θήρᾳ καλοῦ.
[3] Oppian, Cyn. II. 30-42: the translation is very close.

sport, as it marked not only the provision of game
for the table, but also the hunter's triumph in a
contest of wits or speed or strength. Moreover, when
the quarry was a marauding boar, wolf, or bison,
or other dangerous beast, the fierce delight of battle
and victory must prevail over any gentler feeling;
but that such feeling existed among true sportsmen
may be proved by a striking instance. In a passage
quoted above from Xenophon, that writer, speaking
of hare-hunting, makes it part of the joy of the chase
to be in at the death; whereas Arrian shows a very
different spirit. "The aim of true sportsmen[1]
with hounds," he says, " is not to take the hare, but
to engage her in a racing contest or duel, and they
are pleased if she happens to escape. Sometimes
when they view her crouching and trembling with
exhaustion in scanty covert where she has taken
refuge they call off the hounds, particularly if she
has made a gallant fight. I myself many a time,
following the chase on horseback and riding up just
as the hare was captured, have let her go alive;
and if I came too late to save her, I have struck my
forehead in grief[2] that the hounds had slain a gallant
adversary. And here is a point in which I differ
from Xenophon. I agree that to witness the find
and the run in hunting would banish all thought of
one's dearest desire in life: but to see the hare overtaken is neither exciting nor pleasurable: it is plainly
distressing, and not in the least a thing to surpass
the fondest desire of one's heart. But we must
forgive old Xenophon for thinking the capture of
the hare a fine sight, inasmuch as the fast Celtic
hounds of today were unknown to him," and consequently the hare had many more chances of escape.

[1] A literal rendering of the Greek phrase, ὁ τῇ ἀληθείᾳ κυνηγετικός,
and the clearest known expression of the idea in ancient lore.

[2] This expression of grief, not unknown in the West, is common
in the East, and is found over and over again in the Arabian
Nights.

Arrian then, who wrote about 500 years after Xenophon, is often very near in spirit to the modern world; and one may match his language from the Badminton book on hunting, in which the Duke of Beaufort speaks of " the genuine love of the sight of a pack of any hounds in full cry," and remarks also: " The *amari aliquid* inseparable from all sport *surgit* at the death of the hunted animal. There is no more pitiful, more helpless, object than a thoroughly tired-out hare hopping the last fifty yards of her career in front of the pack. Contrast this spectacle with that of a fox beaten to a standstill in the middle of a field, and the leading hound just running into him. We know at least which of the pair *looks* the most afraid."[1] This agreement between the language of the well-bred sportsman of Bithynia and that of the English nobleman, the greatest authority on hunting eighteen hundred years later, is no mere chance coincidence: it shows that the instinct of sport is a common inheritance of the human race in times and countries far sundered, and that the pleasures which it brings—at least to the educated—do not obliterate the finer feelings.[2]

Precisely the same sense of compassion for the hare hunted almost to death is recorded in an anecdote of Archbishop Anselm, who was watching the chase one day when a hare took refuge under his horse and, his gentle tones changing to loud remonstrance, he sternly ordered the hunters to stand and let the hare get away to the woods.[3]

Setting aside now all question or doubt whether the Greeks had within them any real spirit of sport,

---

[1] Hunting (Badminton Library), pp. 82 and 88.
[2] See also Game Pie (Eric Parker), p. 134, on the hare " out of shot."
[3] This story is quoted by the Duke of Beaufort from Green's History of the English People. He gives also many proofs that in the early days of the Church and in the Middle Ages bishops and clerics were lovers of the chase,

one may deal with the qualities required of man and horse and hound in hunting, with the many forms and fashions of the chase, and the varied devices and weapons adopted for its service.

First of all let it be said that the term " hunting " in general and unqualified usage meant to the Greek hare-hunting, just as to us it means fox-hunting. The reason, doubtless, was that hares were more plentiful and more easy to capture than other game; but if it had been a matter of choice and a predilection for that form of sport, few would quarrel with that choice or disparage it today. Indeed, no less a judge than Beckford pronounces that " There is more of true hunting with harriers than with any other description of hounds. . . . In the first place, a hare when found generally describes a circle in her course, which naturally brings her upon her foil, which is the greatest trial for hounds. Secondly, the scent of the hare is weaker than that of any other animal, and, unlike some, it is always worse the nearer she is to her end." One other point in the nature of early Greek hunting must be made quite clear: namely, that in Xenophon's time, for example, hare-hunting did not mean coursing the hare in the open, since open plains were rare, but it meant finding her in bushy or wooded or rough country and driving her towards nets, which had been set beforehand in known runs or other likely places.

The hunter himself must be a young fellow just coming to manhood, and his netsman must be a lad talking Greek, keen on his work, strong and hefty, not only master of his craft but delighting in it. His purse-nets and also his road-nets should be woven from the best flax of Colchis or Egypt or of Carthage—a requirement which shows from what far-sundered places sporting materials were gathered in those days. The hunter must be lightly shod and lightly clad, carry a stout cudgel in his hand, and follow the netsman in silence. Oppian is more explicit. The young hunter, he says, must not be a very heavy man, as he has to be mounted on an active horse accustomed to leap over stone fences and dykes; or, if on foot, he must be light and nimble for forest work: a big, fleshy man would be useless. The body must be lithe, with plenty of muscle, promising swiftness in pursuit and strength in combat with wild beasts, which he may encounter. For weapons the mounted hunter should carry two long lances[1] in his right hand, while he holds the bridle-rein with his left. At his waist he must wear a good hooked hunting-knife[2] both for self-defence and for cutting a passage through thick covert: the hunter on foot will lead a couple of hounds with his left hand. His dress is a shortened tunic, which reaches halfway down to the knees and is kept close by a belt and crossing straps.[3]   A light

[1] As implied in the passage from the Odyssey given above. Specific reference to two spears is given in Il. III. 18; X. 26; XIX. 298, etc.

[2] Prof. Mair renders *hunting-bill*. The Greek is δρεπάνη in Oppian, δρέπανον in Xenophon and Pollux; and Pollux explains that it is needed for clearing bush which would hamper the line of nets. But *bill* suggests too long a handle for a mounted hunter to carry. Moreover, that the hunting-knife was used on the quarry is clear from Seneca's language (Phaedr. 52):

tu jam victor
Curvo solves viscera cultro,

(and one may note that the opening ode of his Phaedra is full of hunting terms). But it may be taken as almost certain that the weapon intended was something like a sickle with only a flat curve, but a sharp edge and point to the blade—exactly like that used by Tutankhamen (see *Illustrated London News* for October 12, 1929).

[3] Here, I think, Prof. Mair has missed the sense in translating " Let him wear a tunic well-girt and fastened above the knee and held tight by crossing straps "—words which must mean that the tunic is strapped to the thigh. The truth is that the skirt of the tunic below the belt was loose, and if " fastened above the knee " would have hampered the hunter at every turn. The crossing straps were on the body of the tunic, and passed over the back of the hunter, and the morses on each shoulder for attachment of the cape may have been fastened on these straps.

cloak with fastening on each shoulder serves as a
protection against bad weather, but can be flung back
and kept in place behind so as to leave the hands
free for action; but it is better to hunt without any
such cape, as it may flap about in a wind, making
a noise which startles the wild animals. So the
tracker whose business it is to follow up dim trails
in the forest should go unshod, lest any sound of
sandal striking a pebble or snapping a twig break
on the slumber of a beast of prey.

It is clear, however, that this counsel of barefoot
movement applied only to the tracker. The hunter
himself could not go among sharp stones or thorn-
bushes without any protection for his feet. No
doubt in the earlier times sandals were worn which
covered little more than the sole of the foot, but it
is quite certain that later something in the nature
of a shoe or boot was used. There is, for example,
in a well-known series of paintings from Pompeii,
a sketch of a cobbler's shop in which winged Amorini
are making boots and shoes, rows of which are
standing on shelves against the wall. It is also
certain that the need of further protection for the
leg than that given by sandals or moccasins led to
the use of gaiters or buskins, which were laced or
fastened with straps, and are often shown in early
works of art. Grattius, writing early in the first
century, speaks of them as part of the hunter's outfit, and he names in addition a fur cap.

So much for the personal equipment or the hunting-
kit of old. But it is strange that so little is said
about the use of bows and arrows. They were
originally perhaps rather Asian than European
weapons, but are commonly represented as part of the
equipment of Artemis (who perhaps for this reason
was called Elaphebolos and Lagobolos), and of the
Amazons; but their use may have been more common
in war than in the chase in early times, though

ARTEMIS ELAPHEBOLOS.
From a vase painting *c.* 500 B.C.

To face page 34.

BOAR HOUNDS.
From a fresco at Tiryns *c.* 1500 B.C.

To face page 25.

paintings and sculptured reliefs often record the
bow as used in hunting.

The Cretans retained their skill in archery for use
in war long after the bow was abandoned by other
Greeks, and formed a special corps. Plato makes
a Cretan explain that the rough mountainous nature
of his country required an equipment of light
weapons and not heavy armour.[1] AElian[2] says that
in his day Cretan bowmen were such good shots
that they could hit wild goats feeding on the top of
a cliff. Moreover, it must always be remembered
that Greek and Roman writers, like those of today,
took for granted facts within the common knowledge
of their readers, and may pass over such facts in
silence; so that we have to learn by accident. Thus
there is no direct record of the bow as a weapon
of the chase in stag-hunting; but Pliny in his account
of the nature and habits of deer remarks on the silly
curiosity which leads them to stare at a horse or a
heifer and not to notice the hunter close at hand, or,
if they see him, to stare at his bow and arrows—[3]
words which prove that Pliny thought of a hunter
as an archer. Even the crossbow[4] was known,
though it does not appear much, if at all, before the
fourth century of our era. Pollux, however, does
mention arrows as part of the hunter's harness, and
sword as well as curved hunting-knife.[5] Finally,
Oppian himself declares that, while he proposes to
write of special kinds of hunting and their appropriate arts or crafts or weapons, he will remark only
briefly upon those things which are in use generally
—such as nets and traps and horses and hounds as
used in the chase; but he adds that hurling the

[1] Legg. I. 625.
[2] V.H. I. 10.
[3] N.H. VIII. 49.
[4] *Arcuballista*—the French *arbalète*. See S. Reinach's Anthro-
pologie, p. 165, for illustration.
[5] Poll. V. 19.

javelin and *close shooting with bow and arrow* are of
customary use in big-game hunting;[1] and he speaks
of the Armenians as renowned for their archery.
The pictorial evidence for the bow in hunting is
abundant.

[1] Cyn. IV. 39-56.

HORSES AND RIDERS.
From the Parthenon.
(Notice the knee-pads.)

To face page 37.

CHAPTER IV

HORSE AND HOUND

Testing a Young Horse—Points of the Horse—Breeds and Colours
—Hounds and their Varieties—Countries and Origins—
Cross-breeding—Points of the Hound—Advances since
Xenophon—Gaulish or Celtic Hound—British and other
Special Hounds.

MUCH less stress is laid by classical writers
on the qualities of the horse than on those
of the hound for purposes of hunting, but only
because the prevailing type of hunting—*i.e.* with
harriers—did not require a very fine breed of horses.
Xenophon has a separate Treatise on Horsemanship
in which he tells one how to judge of a young horse
in buying, and dwells at length on the various points
of the horse. You cannot discover the temper or
manners of an animal which has never been ridden,
but you can judge of his qualities by the build and
conformation of his body. And, remember, there
is a good deal of cheating in horse-dealing. In
looking over a yearling, first of all examine his feet:
if they are unsound he is useless.[1] The hoof must
be solid, rising high fore and aft, so as to keep the
frog[2] off the ground. It must be remembered that
the Greeks never shod their horses,[3] and trusted
to the balance between ordinary growth and ordinary
wear and tear to keep the hoof in good order; moreover, the frog was not cut, any more than the hoof
was pared. A horse with a good hollow foot may

---

[1] This is quite in agreement with Mr. Jorrocks, who puts it,
" No feet, no 'oss," in his less polished language.

[2] The Greek term is χελιδὼν or swallow. See Xen. Hipp. I. 3.

[3] Iron shoes are said to date from about the ninth century.

be known, says Xenophon, by the ring of his hoofs on the ground, like the sound of a cymbal. In this sense of music in the beat of the hoof once again the old world and the new are brought together. In King Henry V. the idea is carried further, where Shakespeare makes the Dauphin say in bragging of his horse: "The earth sings when he touches it: the basest horn of his hoof is more musical than the pipe of Hermes" (Act. III. sc. 7), the bone of the pastern just over the hoof must not be too upright, as that fault renders the rider's seat uncomfortable; nor must it slope too much, as that causes the fetlocks to be galled on rough or stony ground. There must be plenty of bone in the leg, supple knee-joints, powerful shoulders, and a broad chest, which makes for beauty and strength as well as safe action. The neck must not be sagging forward like that of a bear,[1] but arched like the neck of a game-cock; for a horse with such a neck protects his rider, sees well where he is going, and is less liable to bolt. Other points are: head bony, cheek small, eye prominent and not sunken, nostrils wide, crest somewhat large, ears rather small, withers high. The horse must have a good "barrel," loins short and broad, haunches wide and well covered, shoulders high, and a "double back." Here, too, one may quote Shakespeare who in Venus and Adonis gives the points of a good horse as follows:

Round-hoofed, short-jointed, fetlocks shag and
    long,
Broad breast, full eye, small head, and nostril
    wide,
High crest, short ears, straight legs, and passing
    strong,
Thin mane, thick tail, broad buttock, tender hide:
Look, what a horse should have he did not lack.

[1] The English term *ewe-necked* has a different animal comparison, as in the case of the frog.

The meaning of double back is that the spine must not stand out in a ridge, but lie flat between well-developed muscles on either side; and the reason for such a requirement is that the Greeks in Xenophon's time rode bare-back, so that the spine sticking up must make an easy seat impossible. In a later age saddle and harness were in familiar use, and there are in painting and sculpture many figures of horsemen riding with saddle and breast-band or girth, sometimes with a crupper and sometimes without. Finally, says Xenophon, in buying your colt or yearling, remember that the colt with the longest shanks when he is foaled is the most sure for size and stature.

Although a good deal might be written—indeed, has been written[1]—about the various breeds of the horse known in classical times, a few stray notes here alone can be gleaned from that wide field. In prehistoric times the wild horse is said to have been hunted for food and his tail taken home as a trophy. In Homer's day dun horses were freely used for chariots, and Achilles' mount was a dappled dun by the West Wind out of Podarga—names in which it is not fanciful to divine a horse of finest breeding and finest mettle—but it was one remarkable for a long mane, which was left unclipped.[2] In Aristophanes' comedy of The Clouds an iron-grey horse is mentioned as having been purchased by Pheidippides for his wild spendthrift son at the price of twelve minae with money borrowed of a moneylender, Pasion.[3] In the famous chariot-race described by Sophocles[4] there is a list of entries in which the horses are mainly Thessalian. Oppian, in a later age, held that Thessalians were too big for

[1] See Prof. W. Ridgway's Origin and Influence of the Thoroughbred Horse (Cambridge, 1905), to which I am much indebted in this connexion.

[2] Il. XVII. 437.
[3] Ar. Nub. 1225.
[4] Soph. El. 701 *seq.*

hunting; but Thessalian cavalry was far the best in Greece, and from that breed came many of the winners at Olympia. The prevailing colour of the Thessalian was white; Hipponax speaks of white horses of Thrace, and Pindar of white horses of Thebes (Pyth. IX. 83) and of Mycenae (Fr. 216), and white was the colour of one of the teams in Sophocles' chariot-race. But greys were also known in Thessaly, a variation due, as Prof. Ridgway thinks, to crossing with a Libyan stock.[1]

Philip of Macedon (about 350 B.C.) sent both chariot teams and race horses to Olympia, and the

HORSE-RACE: STARTING-POST AND FINISH.
From a Greek vase painting.

winner in the principal flat race was commemorated on an issue of silver tetradrachms,[2] showing the jockey clearly as a boy chosen for his light weight. The news of his victory in the Olympic " Derby " reached Philip at the same time as the news of the birth of his son, Alexander the Great—a double event which must have delighted him. It may be noted that horse-racing had flourished in Greece for three hundred years before King Philip's victory (the first race having been run in 648 B.C., twenty-two years after the first four-horse chariot race): that Alexander's own famous steed, Bucephalus, was a Thessalian: and that much of his success in

1 See Ch. XII. for further reference to this subject.
2 B. Head, Historia Numorum, p. 197.

war came from his use of highly trained heavy cavalry of the same breed.

Further north and west in Europe the horses were of small size, but were not tamed before the close of the Bronze Age. In Britain, at the time of Caesar's invasion, chariots were more in use than cavalry, as the horses were small for riding; and the same usage prevailed in countries north of the Danube, whereas the peoples south of that river had abandoned war chariots by the middle of the fifth century B.C., as Herodotus records. The Romans, however, used chariots in war till about 300 B.C., and long after that date retained them for ceremonial purposes.

Of the Argive horses famed in Strabo's time bay was the best colour, or perhaps chestnut.[1] Oppian gives a long list of breeds famous in the second century, by which time knowledge of the equine race, as developed in many countries round the Mediterranean, was much more widely spread. Cappadocia, Armenia, Scythia, Ionia; Thrace, Achaia, and Elis—Xenophon's country; Crete, Sicily, Tuscany, Mauretania, and North Africa, were all famed for their breeds of horses. The Libyan, says Professor Ridgway, was famed from the dawn of history to the early days of our era for surpassing speed, and he thinks that Spanish or Gaulish or Greek horses noted for the same quality of pace derived it largely from a cross with Libyan bloodstock. The Arab horse does not seem to have been known to Greeks or Romans as possessing special merit: he was probably considered too small.

One may note that the points of a good horse, whether for hunting or for fighting, do not differ materially in Oppian from those in Xenophon. He

---

[1] Aulus Gellius in Noct. Att. III. 9. 3, describes Seius' horse as *magnitudine inusitata, cervice ardua, colore poeniceo—i.e.* a chestnut of remarkable size, carrying his head very high.

must have size and substance and well-knit limbs;
a small head carried high, with a neck arching like
the plume on a helmet; forehead broad, thick curly
forelock; eye clear and fiery, broad chest; and back
with a double chine;[1] a good full tail; muscular
thighs; fine, clean legs; pastern sloping; hoof rising
high, close-grained, and strong. These, says Oppian,
are the qualities prominent in Tuscan, Armenian,
Achaean, and the famous Cappadocian horses; and
such are the horses for hunting wild beasts or for use
as chargers in war. With unflinching courage they
rush on the enemy's serried phalanx: they prick
their ears and are stirred at the call of the trumpet,
nor does their eye quail before " the dense array of
armed warriors, the gleaming bronze, the flashing
sword ": they understand the words of command,
and in siege warfare they aid in bringing up that
sloping roof of shield linked with shield under cover
of which the city walls are approached and battered.
They are the most intelligent of all animals; they neigh
when their rider mounts, and mourn for his death.

Not less admiration for horses is shown in the verse
of another and a better-known poet, Ovid, who
remarks on their proud carriage and noble spirit:
" Their heart knows when victory is won and glories
in winning it. If a horse wins the crown in the
seven laps of a chariot race, with what a lofty air he
carries his head and courts the cheers of the crowd;
or if he comes home (from the chase) decked with
a lion's hide, how superb is his action, how grandly
does he show off his paces, as his hoof tramples the
earth under the weight of his heroic spoils !"[2]

[1] Such is the phrase—ῥαχὶς ἀμφίδυμος. So Verg. Geo. III.
87, *duplex agitur per lumbos spina*. The meaning is given above.
Hayes, quoted by Prof. Mair, speaks of draught horses in which
" the upper muscles of the loin and back stand out as distinct
ridges of muscle on each side of the backbone."

[2] Ovid, Halieutica, a poem of which, unfortunately, only a fragment remains.

THE STIRRUP CUP.

From an Attic Vase c. 400 B.C., in the British Museum.

To face page 42.

But the love of horses was born into the Greeks, and their legends are full of it. Homer tells of the mares sired by the North Wind, Boreas, that " when they coursed over the laden cornfields they ran lightly upon the ears of corn and never brake one; and when they sped over the wide ridges of the sea, they raced on the top of the foaming waves, scarce wetting the hoof ".[1] Bellerophon was carried by his winged horse, Pegasus, above the clouds to encounter and slay the monster Chimaera; and Bucephalus himself passed into later story not merely as the charger of Alexander the Great, but as a fierce combatant in battle against men in armour. Xanthus, the mount of Achilles, is even given a human voice and foretells the death of his master.[2]

This fondness for the horse is as keen in Oppian as in any writer; but when he speaks of the different breeds, the enthusiasm of the moment makes him sometimes difficult to follow. " Of all the breeds nourished by the boundless earth," he says, " the swiftest (ὠκυτάτη) is the Sicilian from the region of Lilybaeum and AEtna."[3] Yet almost in the next line we are told that Armenian and Parthian horses are fleeter (κραιπνότεροι) than the Sicilian, while Iberian[4] horses are a long way in front of the Parthian for speed over the open plain—" swift as the eagle flying, the hawk swooping, or the dolphin cleaving the billows." But these Iberians are good only for a short course: they are small in size and wanting in spirit and endurance; their hoof, accustomed to yielding ground, is too wide and too flimsy; and though they are real beauties to look at, they have no staying-power and are foundered after a run of a few furlongs.

For staying-power the dappled Moorish horse is

[1] Il. XX. 226.   [2] Il. XIX. 404.
[3] Oppian, Cyn. I. 271 *seq.*
[4] Iberia by the Caspian is meant.

unbeaten; but some of the Libyans in the region of
Cyrene come close to him for long-distance running.
In form the two breeds have some resemblance, but
the Libyan is bigger, with a longer body and more
substance, and so can stand heat and thirst better,
and is more fitted for a charger in war. The Tuscan
horse and the huge Cretan have also length of body
and great pace. Oppian repeats himself in saying
that the Sicilian is faster than the Moorish horse
and the Parthian than the Sicilian; but he adds that
the Parthian is a remarkably good-looking animal
with his clear grey eye, and the only horse undaunted
by the roar of a lion. The word κραιπνὸς must
connote hardihood and courage as well as speed; but
even so one can only reconcile these clashing opinions
by adopting the belief that the text has suffered the
loss of a line or other mutilation.[1] The poet is a great
believer in the power of the eye, holding that the
eye of the steed should match the eye of the quarry
in colour—bluish for bears, yellowish for leopards,
fiery and flaming for wild boars, and gleaming grey
for lions.

Two other breeds are commended by Oppian—
the Nesaean from Media, remarkable at once for
exceeding beauty and exceeding docility, and for full
lightish-coloured mane: these are the horses of
kings and princes. The other breed called the
Orynx is also very handsome, and is either marked
all about the neck and back with stripes like a tiger
or is pied all over with round spots like a leopard;
but this latter appearance is produced by branding
and tattooing the very young foals. To us the
striped variety can only suggest the zebra; but the
two are classed together under the one name—Orynx.
Both would seem to be riding-horses, and nothing
is said of their untameable wildness, or of the country
to which they belong, so that they remain rather a

---

[1] See Oppian, Cyn. I. 302, and preceding lines.

mystery.[1] The fancy for the spotted horse is curious; he had a shaggy coat, and the red-hot branding-iron must have seared the skin on the spots permanently —a very cruel business.

It is time now to pass on from horse to hound. That Xenophon in treating of horsemanship is thinking rather of war than of hunting is fairly certain for two reasons—first, that he makes so much of the big Thessalian breed and the Achaean, whereas Grattius, who wrote in the first century A.D., definitely remarks that the heavy Thessalian and Mycenaean breeds are unsuitable for hunting; and next, because Xenophon in his own essay on hunting says little about the horse, but a great deal about the dog. How far Oppian in talking of horses was putting into verse the opinions of Xenophon or giving his own view of the merits of different breeds cannot easily be determined; but there is no question that Oppian was a keen sportsman as well as a poet. In any case those two writers are our best authorities on the hound although they wrote 500 years apart: and if Xenophon, as a country gentleman living on his estate in Elis, had more genuine hound-lore and hunting-lore than Oppian, the Cilician poet, yet during those five centuries the world of sport had not stood still, and Oppian is able to survey a wider field and to record some breeds of hunting-dogs from distant countries unknown, or scarcely known, to Xenophon. Thus, whereas Xenophon names only two varieties of hounds, both Laconian or Spartan, as used for hunting the hare, Indian for deer, and Indian, Cretan, Locrian, and Laconian for wild-boar, Oppian gives a list of sixteen breeds, which include the famous Celtic or Gaulish hound (not a greyhound, as some imagine, and not heard of in Xenophon's

---

[1] The colts branded are called *baby colts*, νηπίαχοι, and they must have been bred in captivity, so that no sort of wild horse can be in question.

day), dogs from Iberia,[1] Umbria, Locris, Thrace, Scythia, Magnesia, Amorgos, and shepherds' dogs on the banks of the Nile. Grattius says that the Umbrian is faithful and keen-nosed: if only he were staunch in the fray! And the world of Grattius is wider. The Mede, he notes, is a wild fighter. The breed of Gelonus is clever but cowardly; Persians are clever and courageous too; even Chinese (*i.e.* Thibetan) dogs are bred; and Hyrcanians are said to cross with tigers. Such a cross-bred will take a heavy toll of your cattle; but keep him, and he will atone for all his sins at home by his gallant behaviour at close quarters in the forest. One may add that Nicander traces the Indian breed back to the hounds of Actaeon, and by an even bolder flight of fancy derives the Molossians from the bronze hounds with life breathed into them as forged by Hephaestus.[2]

Xenophon's two classes of Laconians were called the *badger* and the *fox* respectively—names given from some physical resemblance, and not, of course, from their use in the field, though Xenophon thinks that the *badger* was so called because Castor, who had a passion for hunting, carefully preserved this breed, and that the *fox* variety was a cross between dog and fox. The *badger* was a much bigger hound than the *fox*, and so could be run after larger game like wild-boar.

Crossing hounds was well understood. Oppian recommends a cross of Iberian with Scythian or Saramtian, Tuscan with Laconian, Arcadian with Elean, Carian with Thracian, Cretan with Paeonian, if crossing is wanted: nevertheless it is far better to

---

[1] Cyn. I. 371 *seq.* Prof. Mair thinks that *Iberian* here means Spanish. It may be so, but the Iberia on the west coast of the Caspian seems more likely, as it was specially famed like Albania (*i.e.* Georgia) for its breed of powerful dogs. It is clear that the name *Iberia* for Spain was recent in Strabo's time from his words ἥσπερ νῦν 'Ιβηρίας καλοῦμεν (Geog. 199).

[2] Pollux, V. 38-9.

keep the several breeds pure, if the aim is to provide
the best possible hound for the chase. But the breeds
specified are only a few: there are thousands of them,
he says, and Grattius also says they come from a
thousand different regions. As an instance Pollux
remarks that there were two special breeds of Cretan
hounds called respectively διάπονοι and πάριπποι—
words not easy to render in good English; we might
perhaps call them forwards, or outworkers, and by-
runners. The business of the forwards was to follow
a likely trail at great speed and unaccompanied,
overtaking and engaging the quarry. Sometimes
they would even keep going through the night,
sleeping near the game, and renewing the battle in
the morning. The by-runners had to run close
alongside the mounted hunter, neither before nor
after, and presumably they guided him on the line
taken by the wild beast and the forward-working
hounds.[1]

However, the characteristics of the several species
are seldom painted with any clearness, though the
general points required in the hunting-dog are set
out and more or less agreed. Size is the first requirement: the head should be light and well-knit, with
flat nose,[2] a long mouth with mischievous-looking
teeth; eyes with a lift, dark and shining; forehead
broad with a deep division; ears small and hairless
at the back; neck long, loose, and well rounded;
shoulder-blades somewhat outstanding; chest broad
and well covered; the ribs must never fall low, but
should lessen in depth from the forelegs, which are
shorter than the hindlegs: haunches should be full,
but not too fleshy: tail long, straight, and thin.
That is the type of hound for handsome appearance, shapely form, activity, and speed; and such

[1] Poll. V. 40. Seneca, Phaedr. I. 34, speaks of *pugnaces Cretes*
straining at the leash.

[2] σιμή as opposed to γρυπή, or hook-nosed (like a vulture).

hounds will have a good mouth and a bright, cheery look.

Arrian, who lived before Oppian was born and whose Essay on Hunting has been already cited, was a remarkable person—historian, military writer, geographer, traveller, and sportsman: he opens his Essay with a critique of Xenophon which is worth giving here.

Xenophon, he writes, has spoken fully of the advantages of hunting, and has shown how men brought up and trained in the field have been highly favoured of heaven and have been held in honour throughout Greece. He has shown, too, the relation of the art of hunting to the art of war, the time of life, the habit of body, and the type of character required in practice; also the way of setting stake-nets, purse-nets, and blocking-nets.[1] He has written of hares and their habits, their feeding-grounds, and their legs, and of the way to discover them: of hounds too, those clever and those useless at following a trail, and of the way to judge hounds by their appearance and their performance. Something, moreover, he has written on the hunting of boars and stags, lions and bears, and ingenious devices for capturing them. But there are short-comings in his essay, due not to any careless writing, but to the fact that the Gaulish breed of hounds, and also the Scythian and Libyan breeds of horses, were then unknown.[2] These defects I will make good: for I bear the same name as Xenophon, belong to the same country, and from my early days have been keen about the same things—war and sport and intellectual interests. And in this I but follow Xenophon, who in like manner set out in the Essay on Horsemanship the defects of

[1] *I.e.* nets set across known runs of game.
[2] This statement about the horses is very questionable. See Ch. XII below.

Simon, his predecessor, and that not in any spirit of controversy, but in desire for the advancement of useful knowledge.

Xenophon knew nothing of Europe except the Greek settlements in Italy and some places made familiar by commerce; and his unacquaintance with the Celtic or Gaulish harrier is proved by his saying that the hare is never run down by hounds unless it be by some mishap or accident; whereas Gaulish harriers of good breed and good heart always capture the hare unless she runs across very bad country—forest or ravine—or unless a big dyke allows her to slip away unseen. Moreover, in Xenophon it is always driving to nets, or if the hare happens to avoid being netted she must be chased till she gives in from sheer exhaustion. This, says Arrian, was the style of hunting in vogue also in Caria and in Crete. The Gaulish hound is just as good as the Carian and the Cretan in working out a scent: but incomparably swifter, though *rough and wild in appearance*—a remark which shows that it is altogether a mistake to identify the breed with the greyhound of today, which depends on sight, has no nose for scent, and is smooth-coated, slim, and graceful in appearance. All three breeds throw their tongues too freely, following a trail with clamorous baying; but the Gaulish are the most excited at the find, and often fail to distinguish a fresh run of the hare from the worn foil to her form. The Gaul is very quick at turning, yet very apt to overrun the scent by reason of his speed—so much so that the hunter is often well content on a winter's day if he comes home with a single hare.[1] These hounds are called also Egousians, from the name of

---

[1] Caesar notes the devotion of the Gallic people to hunting: *vita omnis in venationibus consistit* (B.G. VI. 21); whereas Tacitus of the Germanic tribes says, *Quoties bella non ineunt, multum venationibus, plus per otium transigunt* (Germ. 15): so that war came first with the Germans, hunting first with the Gauls.

the Celtic tribe among which they were bred and became famous: but the Celtic name was οὐέρ-τραγος, from a word meaning *fleet-foot*, and this Martial turns into *vertagus* in an epigram, in which he says that the Celtic hound, on seizing the hare, retrieves it uninjured for his master.[1] (There seems no other mention of the Celt as a retriever.) But it must be repeated that the breed are rough-haired and ugly-looking, and the better their pedigree the worse are their looks, so that there is a popular proverb among the Gauls comparing them to beggars by the wayside; for they speak with a melancholy, whining voice and follow the chase with tones of whimpering and entreaty rather than fierce clamour.

On the points of the dog generally Arrian for the most part agrees with Xenophon's canon; but he does not think it matters much whether a hound is hook-nosed or snub-nosed, or rate highly the requirement of good sinew under the forehead. Length of body is essential, and there is no more certain criterion for breed and speed in every variety of hound: you may see a hound with faults all over, but if he is long in the body he has generally plenty of spirit and pace. Size, too, is often good in itself, and some hounds, with little else to recommend them, seem to derive a better nature from their mere size. Eyes should be large, clear, and bright: the best sort are fiery and flashing for big-game hunting: next come black, with a look of fierceness: and third bluish-grey. Grey eyes are not a bad sign.

" I once had a hound," he says, "with the deepest possible blue-grey eyes, very quick, fond of work, full of spirit, and sure of foot, so that she could

---

[1] Ep. XIV. 200:

> Non sibi sed domino venatur vertagus acer,
> Illaesum leporem qui tibi dente feret.

Lemaire quotes a ridiculous derivation—quasi *fertrahus*—i.e. *ferum trahens*.

account for four hares in a day's sport. She is
a most gentle creature (for I still have her with
me as I write), and most fond of company, and I
never knew any other dog so devoted to my friend
and fellow-huntsman, Megillus. When the day's
run was over she never left him or me for a moment.
She stays with me if I happen to be indoors, comes
alongside when I go out, follows me to the gym-
nasium, lies down while I am stripping, and on my
way home she goes in front, often looking back to
make sure that I have not taken some side turning:
then finding all well she brightens and goes on merrily
ahead again. If I have to go out on some city
business, she remains with Megillus and behaves
in exactly the same way with him. If either of us
happens to be ailing she never quits him. On
seeing one of us after a short absence she jumps up
gently in welcome, and cries welcome too in most
friendly fashion. When we are at dinner she mouths
one or the other of us by the foot, as a hint that
she should have her portion. She has more language
than any other dog I ever knew, and can always
tell you what she wants. Thus she was once
whipped, when she had puppies, and to this day
if anyone uses the word *whip* she goes to the speaker,
crouches down begging, and puts her mouth up to
be kissed; then jumping up with a grin she puts her
paws on his shoulders, and will not release him
till all signs of threatening temper have vanished.
I should be quite willing to put on record the name
of my dog as a memorial, just as Xenophon of Athens
had a dog, remarkable for speed and cleverness and
good manners, which was called Fling (Hormé)."[1]
Lovers of the dog will not quarrel with this lively

[1] Corresponding more nearly to the too familiar *Dash* perhaps.
It is the last in Xenophon's list of hound names, and there is no
exact English equivalent. The French *élan* gives the sense
admirably.

sketch of Arrian's pet hound—a sketch in which I have followed the original Greek with studied closeness. It gives just one of those intimate pictures of life in classic times—pictures which, like the discoveries at Troy and Mycenae, Knossos, Luxor, Kish, and above all at Pompeii, tend to dispel the strange mists which a dull imagination sees brooding over the dim peoples of antiquity, and it brings home to us across the ages something of that touch of nature which proves the whole world kin.

Of the points of the hound, as regards shape and make, little more need be said; but as regards colour, a really curious coincidence between ancient and modern opinion is worth remarking. Arrian says —τὰ δὲ χρώματα οὐδὲν διοίσει ὁποῖα ἂν ἔχωσι— colour is unimportant—and in the Badminton Hunting the Duke of Beaufort, speaking also of harriers, uses identically the same words, "Colour is unimportant,"[1] but blue-mottled the best. Arrian mentions black, white, and tan,[2] as prevailing colours, and that a motley was usual is shown by his statement that a uniform colour does not necessarily denote a throw-back to the wild:[3] he adds that, whatever the colour, it must be clear and bright, and the coat, whether rough or smooth, must be fine and close and silky. Here, then, we have it that both rough-haired and smooth-haired hounds of various colour were used as harriers: and here is another point of agreement with Badminton, which says,[4] "There is no distinct breed of harriers now and probably never was," though dwarf foxhounds are often used: they have, however, too much dash, and when

---

[1] Page 77.

[2] πυρραί.

[3] This is said in direct contradiction of Xenophon, Cyn. 4. 7, who considered the single colour underbred; the black or the tan should have a white patch on the head, and the white should have a dark patch.

[4] Page 74.

the hare doubles and manœuvres, they keep over-running the scent.

On the point of colour, however, Oppian is quite at variance with his predecessor Arrian, though apparently he is thinking rather of big-game hounds than of harriers. For he remarks that a bright white and a blue-black are both extremely bad, as hounds so coloured are unable to stand summer sun or winter's snow: while the best colouring resembles that of wild animals—wolves, tigers, foxes, or leopards—and a good tawny colour bespeaks swift-ness and strength.[1] In the remarkable fresco from Tiryns the large boar-hounds, which are of one type and fine race, have light-coloured bodies with patches of black, dark red, or blue: they carry their collars in the hunt.[2]

It is needless to dwell further on the points of the hound. Arrian has a general remark[3] that the best dog is one of good size and clean build which resembles the bitch in suppleness; while the best bitch is one which with its air of race and good muscle resembles the dog. But Oppian always speaks of the dogs used in the chase as bitches—no doubt an overstatement—and the hare is always a male to the Greek sportsman, in contrast to the usage in our hunting-lore. One may regret that characteristics of the special breeds of hounds are seldom if ever drawn with a clear precision enabling us to identify them. The names which conveyed everything to the sportsman of old come to us for the most part with a blurred meaning: they give a picture in outline to be filled by fancy. But that is not always the fault of the writers. Naturally enough breeds and classes of hounds have changed

[1] Oppian, Cyn. I. 427-436. *Cappy* in the hunting song had
  " His tail pitcher-handled, his colour jet black."
[2] See illustration, p. 25.
[3] Arrian, Cyn. VI. 2.

in two thousand years: many breeds known to Greeks
and Romans have passed into degenerate mongrels
and been lost to the world; while other sorts, by
care and selection, have been gradually moulded to
a higher type, or have branched into new varieties.
It seems then that it would be idle to spend labour
on any general identification, but the difficulties may
be judged from one or two particular examples.

Pliny[1] tells the story of a very powerful and very
rare hound which was given by the King of Albania,
i.e. Georgia, to Alexander the Great when on his
march to India. Alexander, much pleased with the
huge size of the dog, had bears, wild-boars, and stags,
loosed in front of him, but he lay on the ground
with a look of immovable disdain; and Alexander,
angered by such a combination of laziness and
strength, ordered him to be killed. Hearing of this,
the King of Albania sent him another hound, saying
that this was the last of the breed in his possession,
and advising Alexander not to worry him again with
small game, but to try him with a lion or elephant.
First a lion was produced, encountered, and crushed:
then an elephant was brought forward, at the sight
of which the bristles stood up all over the hound
and he bayed with a voice of thunder. He engaged
the beast, leaping on him whenever he saw an
opening, circling round him, and using the most
scientific tactics in assault and retreat, until the
monster reeled and fell with a crash which shook
the ground. We ask in vain whether a hound of
this type was something quite exceptional even for
Albania and Iberia; or was it only an exceptional
specimen of the known Iberian breed? Pollux[2]
tells a somewhat similar story of a hound lent by
Sopeithes to Alexander on trial: but here the hound,
though showing the same contempt for small game,
was not killed, but seized a lion and held on, wrestling

[1] N.H. VIII. 61.   [2] V. 42.

with it till it fell outmatched and was given the
coup de grâce by a hunter's knife. Perittas, another
Bactrian hound, which cost Alexander a hundred
minae, not only killed a lion but had a city founded
in his honour, and named after him, by his proud
master. A hound which conquered lions—κύων
λεοντοδάμας—is named by Pindar (Fr. 53).

Again, one of the most highly prized breeds of
sporting dog in the Old World was the British hound,
which was probably known in Europe before the
Roman invasion, because Strabo, after remarking
that well-bred hunting-dogs are exported from
Britain, adds that the Celts (or Gauls of North-
Western France) use them in war as well as in the
chase.[1] So Grattius says, " Cross over to Britain,
and you will find a rich reward (at great expense)
if, in choosing your hound, you think less of good
form and good looks, which are deceptive: for when
the great day of battle comes, and the shout of Mars
rings from the height of deadly peril, then "—your
grand Molossian, Acarnian, and the rest, will fade
in comparison with the British dog of war.[2] Nemesianus calls him very useful for hunting, and so far
one imagines a fierce big dog, something of the mastiff
breed. On the other hand Oppian describes him
as small, though worthy of great renown in song.[3]
He is called by the Britons the *Agassaean*, and in
size resembles the worthless and greedy house-dog:
is very lean and rough-haired, eye dull, feet rounded
with formidable claws, and mouth armed with rows
of close-set venomous teeth. But this Agassaean
has the best nose of any hound for tracking, and can
carry the scent in the air as well as on the ground.

[1] Geog. 199.

[2] Grattius, I. 174 *seq*. War dogs are mentioned by AElian
(V.H. 14-46) as used by the people of Magnesia in fighting against
the Ephesians; they were launched as the first line of attack.

[3] Oppian, Cyn. I. 468-480. It seems difficult to sever
μεγάλης from ἀοιδῆς, as Professor Mair does; but the sense is not
in doubt.

Not a word here about his use in war, though war was less common in Oppian's day: and the comparison in size with a house-dog is about as useful as saying that he was as big as a stone.

Nor is it possible to reconcile these various points in the English hound of the first century. One is tempted at one moment to picture a bloodhound or mastiff of noble race—Claudian describes him as able to break the neck of a bull[1]—at the next perhaps some kind of wolf-hound,[2] but one is baulked at almost every turn of opinion. This only is clear: he was a first-class fighting dog with a first-rate nose: for the rest, conjecture and blank uncertainty. One may perhaps hazard a guess that he was not far removed from the old Welsh hound, from which the modern foxhound is partly derived. It may be, however, that the Norwegian elkhound is today the nearest representative of the type: too large possibly, but a splendid animal, splendidly accomplished at his work, keen of scent, a most scientific ranger, and a determined fighter at bay. No one who, like myself, has seen him hunting will think this picture overdrawn.

But it is worth noting that the two chief points of the old English Agassaean find their parallel in the Molossian, which was famed all over the Greek and Roman world for strength and courage, as well as for tracking: as shown in the familiar line of Sophocles—

κυνὸς Μολοσσῆς ὥς τις εὔρινος βάσις

—like some Molossian keenly on the scent.

[1] Stil. III. 301: *Magnaque taurorum fracturae colla Britannae* Is there any tradition of this in our term bull-dog ? Daremberg identifies the Agassaean with the bull-dog, but I have shown this to be quite impossible.

[2] Or boar-hound. Orelli records an inscription found in Britain—*Silvano invicto sacrum ob aprum eximiae formae captum quem multi antecessores praeclari non potuerunt*—a huge boar which had long baffled the finest hunters of the day.

DEER-HOUND.
From a Pompeian painting.

To face page 57.

The examples above given are typical of many other cases in which perplexity arises from similar looseness of description.   Here and there, however, while literary records are wanting in precision, pictorial records, such as wall-paintings and drawings on vases or panels of sculpture, preserve an image of hunter and hound at a particular place or period. These drawings and sculptures are unquestionably true to nature, and so far valuable, although they help but little towards the definition of the several breeds of hounds named in classical writings.

Greek literature is much richer than Roman in hunting-lore: but it is certain that Ovid had nearly as fine a sense of sportsmanship and as great a love of the hound as his contemporary Arrian.   Unfortunately the poem of Ovid on which this statement is founded remains but as a charming and tantalising fragment[1]—an unfortunate accident, when a vast amount of his writing survives, some of which could better be spared.   But this is what he says about hounds:

" Of hounds what praise comes foremost ?   See their headlong daring, their clever hunting, their power in the chase !   How they snuff the wind with nostrils lifted up to catch a scent; then, nose to ground, they give tongue on finding it, and rouse the hunters at their cry."

One cannot imagine Vergil as keen on the chase, but he tells the farmer that his dogs must not be the last thing he has to look after: that the Laconian or Spartan breed, with its renown for swiftness, and the bold Molossian must be brought up together on whey: that with them on guard he need have no fear of cattle-lifters by night, or raiding wolves, or brigands.   Often, too, he can chevy wild asses, hunt hare or deer, start the wild boar from his lair in the forest and harry him to the baying of his hounds;

[1] His Halieutica.

or on the mountain heights he can drive a giant
stag onward towards the nets to the chorus of their
music.[1]

One cannot suppose Vergil here mistaken; but it
is rather surprising that he speaks of hunting wild
asses in Italy as almost an everyday occurrence.
However, the Roman farmer or country gentleman
had his sporting dogs and his sporting tastes as
well as the Greek. Moreover, the Gaulish or Celtic
hound was naturally as familiar to lovers of the
chase in the west as in the eastern parts of the
Mediterranean.[2] Claudian neatly sums up the three
chief excellences of hounds in a few words:

illae gravioribus aptae
Morsibus: hae pedibus celeres: hae nare sagaces,[3]

i.e. tackling-power, pace, and keenness of nose.
But there is no better description of a good hunting-
dog than that in the Anthology:

τὸν κύνα τὸν πάσης κρατερῆς ἐπιΐδμονα θήρης

—the hound who kenned all noble hunting lore.[4]

---

[1] Verg. Georg. III. 404-413, is here closely followed.
[2] See, for example, Martial, III. 47. 11: laporemque laesum
Gallici canis dente.
[3] Stil. III. 298.
[4] Anth. P. VI. 175.

CHAPTER V

AT WORK IN THE FIELD

Names, Characters, and Manners of Hounds—Behaviour in the
Field—A Run with Harriers—Seasons and Scent—Hunting
at Night—Training of Hounds—Sport in Gaul—Arrian and
the Chase.

JUST as now in the twentieth century, so
two thousand four hundred years ago every
hound had a name to which he answered. Names,
says Xenophon, must be given at the puppy stage,
and must be short for quick calling. He sets out
a very long list of such names, all dissyllabic, and
mostly nouns substantive where we should use the
adjective: thus Heart for Hearty, Strength for
Sturdy, Haste for Hasty: but Lance, Croaker,
Bustler, Crafty, and others, would sound well enough
from a huntsman today. And most of the names
bestowed denote some point of character desired
by the owner in his hound. Readers of Shakespeare
will remember Holdfast,[1] Merriman, Clowder, Silver,
and Belman.

For character was at least as important as form
for the field. Hounds with a sullen look for all
comers are underbred.[2] Better are those ill-disposed
to strangers, but fond of their own masters. You
may have known a hound moping, lying about the
place, with a dull and dispirited air, pleased with
nothing and nobody, yet, when he was taken out to
hunt, wild with joy, and by his radiant greeting to

[1] Henry the Fifth, II. 3: the other names occur in the Taming of
the Shrew
[2] Arrian, Cyn. VII. 1.

59

everybody and engaging manners he proved that he
was merely bored by sitting at home. Now that is a
good sign. The best hounds are friendly to all, and
like the sight of a man. Those that are afraid of
men, nervous, and alarmed without rhyme or reason,
are underbred. Those, too, are no good which,
when slipped in the field, refuse to come to heel
when bidden, but scurry about, regardless of a quiet
call and scared away by a stern word of command.[1]

Hounds vary in action when casting for the scent.
Some on finding the line go ahead mute, without a
sign: others move their lugs only without waving
sterns, while some keep their ears still, with sterns
waving. Some again prick up their ears and run
frowning along the line, sterns tucked down; while
others behave quite differently, fling madly round
the line when found, give tongue, and trample out
the scent. Another sort will make a very wide cast,
get ahead of the line, overrunning the hare, then will
hit off the line and begin fumbling and guessing:
they may then view the hare in her form, and stand
still all a-quiver waiting for the hare to move.

A hound that forges ahead and casts about for a
find when others have made it shows want of confidence: one that overruns the scent is ill-bred. A
lot of them give up and wander home. Then there
are the " babblers," who upset the hunt by throwing
their tongues for nothing. Others run off to a shout
anywhere in the field, instead of sticking to their
work, or show utter want of intelligence, or take wild
fancies. There are also " skirters " or " ringers ";
and " shirkers," who scamper straggling about off
the line, and make a mere pretence of hunting.

One must repeat here that Xenophon thought of
hare-hunting in connection with netting, and had
little or no purpose of running down the quarry in
the open. This is curiously shown by his remark

[1] This is from Arrian: what follows is from Xenophon.

that hounds should be taken more often to the
mountains than to farm lands, because it is much
easier to track and follow up a hare on the fells, as
the arable is full of game paths. Quite apart from
better hunting, however, hill country gives the hounds
better exercise and tends to keep their feet sound.
The netsman must be lightly clad as he sets out with
his purse-nets, which he must stake in winding
ways and in rough, steep places, ravines, and torrent-
beds, or the like, leaving openings here and there.
This must be done at peep of day, not before, for
fear of scaring the hare off her form. There is a
cord for pulling when the hare is netted, but
care must be taken to pull so that she does not
escape.

While the nets are being set, the hounds are held
each on a single slip; and, when the nets are ready,
the netsman remains on guard watching while the
hunter goes to drive for the quarry and slips one
hound, his cleverest tracker. As soon as there
is a find, the other harriers are slipped one at a time,
and the hunter follows cautiously, calling on them
severally by name, but restrainedly, so as not to
excite them prematurely. Joyous and eager, forward
they run, picking up one line and then another
out of the tangle; swinging, throwing up, and flinging
to recover the scent, racing along one in front of
another, sterns waving, ears drooping, and eyes
flashing.

When they are close to their quarry, they do not
leave the hunter in doubt, with their body a-quiver
from muzzle to stern, as they rush like warriors to the
onslaught,[1] vieing in speed, bunching, spreading,
and forward all again. So they come up to the hare
sitting in her form. Up she springs and away,
leaving all the clatter and clamour of hounds behind

---

[1] πολεμικῶς ἐπιφερόμεναι. Here again is the image of war, and
Mr. Jorrocks is justified again.

her. Then let the hunter shout "Youi, youi,[1] forrard away, hounds! Oh, well done! Oh, clever, clever!" The hare is soon lost to view, but she generally doubles back, and makes a ring towards the lay where she was found, and she may be taken there. But if not, the hunter, who has been racing on foot, must lift the hounds and look for another. Or the hounds come on the same line again, and as they own the scent, he cries out, "Well done, hounds! After her, hounds! Follow on, follow on!" If they get so far ahead that he has no chance of coming up with them, or he has lost his bearings, or if they are somewhere near at hand, working out the line very surely but out of sight, he shouts to any man he happens to come across, "Hullo, there! have you seen the hounds?" Learning what has happened, he may find them on the line again, when he will stand by and cheer them on, calling every hound by name and using every note in his voice. Thus, if the hunt is all among mountain paths, he must sing out, "Yohe, hounds, Yohe!" as that sound carries far. If they are at fault, straggling from the line and overrunning, "Come back, hounds!" is the cry, and they must be swung round, casting till they own the scent again. Then away they go in a flurry, but work together and pass signs to each other, the hunter following cautiously. As they near the quarry they jump over each other in the press, and throwing their tongues look up at the hunter to tell him that this is the real business. The hare then may be driven into the nets, or pulled down in a fair run in the open, or knocked over in some hiding-place by the good stout stick or club which the hunter carries.

Such is Xenophon's account of a run with his harriers about 400 B.C. Though I have somewhat

---

[1] The Greek ἰώ is almost identical here with Mr. Jorrocks' *Youi*,

altered his arrangement to piece the story together as it stands, yet the rendering of the original Greek into English is so close as to be almost word for word: and one cannot fail to be struck with the manifold correspondence of the ideas and language of the chase with those prevailing today. Naturally, however, there are differences of practice to notice. It has already been shown that the setting of nets, towards which the hare had to be manœuvred, was essentially a part of the game in Xenophon's time, whereas in later days the Gaulish breed of hounds had been discovered which, by their combination of great speed and elastic movement, could contend on more equal terms with the hare and run her down in the open.[1]

Other points to remark are first, that in the picture given above the sportsman is on foot, and not mounted—a fact which may be mainly due to the rough nature of the country which Xenophon was accustomed to hunt: next, that there is no mention of any *company* of hunters, such as gathers at a meet of hounds nowadays, and further there is no mention even of a companion in the chase, though that omission is probably accidental. Hunt servants there are—for looking after the nets and for holding several couples of hounds on leash. Numbers are not given. One may, however, be tolerably certain that not less than six couple of hounds were taken out for a day in the field: and one must suppose that the men leading the hounds in slip helped in some way to control the pack when they were running, although there is no hint in the Greek text of anything like a huntsman, or whipper-in, or whip, so that the hunter himself acts as master and manages the hounds solely, it would seem, by the use of his

[1] Xenophon speaks of young Cyrus as using (1) tracking dogs to find the hare; (2) coursing hounds to run the hare; and (3) nets to stop the hare if she gets away (Cyr. I. 6, 40).

voice: for there is no record of calling on or calling off hounds by a horn. This omission of all mention of a horn is curious. Daremberg and Saglio in their learned work[1] hold that hounds were trained by whistle, basing their opinion on a passage in Aristophanes:[2] but the passage contains not the smallest warrant for any such theory and merely describes a man setting his dogs on an enemy by hissing between his teeth, as the words show:

$$\text{ὅταν οὗτός γ' ἐπισίζῃ}$$
$$\text{ἐπὶ τῶν ἐχθρῶν τιν' ἐπιρρύξας ἀγρίως αὐτοῖς ἐπιπηδᾷς}$$

Moreover Pollux expressly refutes any such interpretation by defining ἐπισίζειν when used of hounds as μετά τινος ἀσήμου φωνῆς ἐφεῖναι, *i.e.* by a vocal sound without words,[3] and no instrumental sound is here possible. But more about the horn will be found in a later chapter. Two things, however, are quite plain—the hunter is conceived of as a gentleman hunting his own pack for sport; and master, men, and hounds all share in the intense excitement and enjoyment of the chase.

With the exception of heavy snow and hard frost, all seasons seem to have been considered suitable for hunting, and a distinction is drawn between hounds which could stand the great heat in summer and those which flagged or fell out altogether. Yet in hot weather hounds were stopped by rule at midday and taken home, or given a long rest. In spring mid-day or afternoon were good times: mid-day was to be avoided in autumn: but on a winter's day any hour might be chosen.

On conditions of scent past and present ideas are not wholly in agreement—probably for the very good reason that the facts differed. In winter, says

---

[1] Dictionnaire des Antiquités Grecques et Romaines (Paris, v.d.), s.v. Venatio.
[2] Vesp. 704.   [3] Poll. V. 10.

Xenophon, the scent of the hare lies longer, as the long night keeps her at home more: but with a frost there is no scent in the early morning, and hounds have their noses numbed also, so that nothing can be done till a thaw sets in.   A heavy dew keeps the scent down and heavy irregular showers draw it off. Worse still are rains with a southerly wind, which drown the scent (a view which John Peel would denounce with some vigour), but cool northerly winds hold it together.   By clear moonlight scent is at its best: for the hares revel in the light, playing together and leaping up in the air; but if a fox crosses the scent, he stains it.   The mild equable temperature of spring tends to produce a warm clear scent, except where patches of violets and other early flowers taint the scent with their odours. (One has heard something very like this in modern times, with an uncomplimentary epithet in front of *violets*.)   Summer is not a good season for scent: the scent does not lie well: moreover the hound's nose is less keen, for the heat makes a hound slack and limp all over.   The best of all seasons is the autumn, when crops have been gathered in, weeds are dead, and there is no smell from plants or flowers to mingle with clean scent and foul it.[1]

A hare on the run does not leave so lasting a scent as one on the way home to her form, as in the latter case she lops along more slowly and keeps stopping, so that the scent is more closely concentrated.   In woody places also it is stronger than in open ground, because, as she passes along or sits up, she keeps brushing against things.   When the ground burgeons with the growth of springtime, she prefers the fields to the mountains: but wherever she happens to be, there she sits when the hounds are after her, unless she has a sudden scare by night.

[1] The terms εὔοσμος and δύσοσμος were used of good and bad hunting scent.

Is this another allusion to hunting at night ? The
chase by moonlight was mentioned above, though
one would think it a rather rare event. Yet Words-
worth has the same idea from whatever source he
derived it, when, speaking of the Greek imagination
and love of nature, he depicts the " nightly hunters' "
appeal to Artemis, as

> the goddess with her nymphs
> Across the lawn and through the darksome grove
>
>   *   *   *   *   *
>
> Swept in the storm of chase.[1]

It is useless to take out hounds which are off their
feed, or when a strong wind is blowing to scatter the
scent: but as a rule they may be hunted every other
day. When starting out to find a hare, it is well to
try the cultivated land first, and for those that keep
off the farms, try meadow and vale, stream, stone-
brash, or woody places. If a hare is put up, do not
shout, or the hounds may become too madly excited
to own the scent. Mountain hares are the fastest:
next come those of the plain: while those of marsh
land are the slowest. Hares accustomed to every
sort of country give the best sport and take the most
killing. They like to run up hill, if possible, as
their hindlegs are longer than the fore. They are
easily seen when crossing ploughland or stubble or
level roads: but, when running over stony ground or
among scrub, they are often protected by their
colour. If a hare is well ahead of the hounds, she
will stop and sit bolt upright, watching and listening
for their baying or the noise of their running, and will
shape her course accordingly.

Xenophon has further notes on the training of
hounds for the field. Dog hounds may be taken out
at ten months old, bitches at eight: but they must

---

[1] Excursion, IV. 869. The chase by night is also mentioned by
Plato in the passage given above.

HARE AND HOUND.
From a Pompeian painting.

To face page 67.

be on long leashes and made to keep near the trackers. When a hare is found, promising puppies must not be slipped before she has got ahead and is out of sight: for they must learn to follow the scent, and not to rush in at view. As soon as they begin to slacken. throwing up and spreading, call them off: they must never be allowed to get into a bad habit of that sort, but must be taught to follow up the line till the hare is taken.

Other remarks upon the treatment and education of hounds are found elsewhere. There is mention of a freshly killed hare being dragged along the ground in a crooked course and then buried, to give the young hounds a lesson in tracking. Arrian talks about their diet and diseases, and says they must be kept tied up as a rule, otherwise they will get restive when on the slip and gnaw at the leather. For the full-grown hound one meal a day—towards evening—is enough.

He has, however, more about the hare. He agrees that good hounds must not be slipped close to the hare nor more than one couple at a time. If she is a very fleet hare which has run the gauntlet a score of times, you must not startle her from her form with a sudden clamour of hounds, which will set her heart throbbing. In this way unfortunately the hare is often " chopped ": or, as Arrian more picturesquely puts it, " many a noble hare has perished ingloriously without any deed of daring and without any achievement worthy of renown "—language which, with its mock-heroic style, Mr. Jorrocks might have found rather beyond him, though once again the image of war is stamped upon it.[1] But you must give her a chance to get away and recover her wits: then if she wants a run, she cocks her ears and springs up with a leap, and away goes

[1] Cicero also remarks that hunting has a sort of resemblance to war training—*bellicae disciplinae similitudinem.*

the hunt, straining every limb to follow the line.
Now you have a sight that will more than reward you
for all the pains you have taken with your hounds.

The most valiant hares are those that lie out and
harbour in open country. They are too bold to
think of concealment: indeed, to judge by all appearance, they challenge the hounds to combat.[1] In
the pursuit they disdain to retreat into hollows or
copses, if there are any at hand to furnish an easy
escape from danger, but they charge along the plain,
defying hounds. If the hounds are slow movers,
the hare trots along at the same pace: but if hounds
are fast, she puts out all her powers. Often, too,
when hares have taken to the level and find a first-
rate hound so close at heel as almost to overshadow
them, they throw him off by continually doubling
and twisting, and then make for the ravines, if they
know of any path leading downwards. This now is
the sign and token of victory for the hound.

Here follows in Arrian the passage which I have
already given in connexion with the question of
hunting for the sake of exercise and sport as distinguished from hunting for the sake of killing the
quarry[2]—a passage which need not be repeated but
which further brings into prominence Arrian's idea
of the chase as a kind of chivalrous warfare.

Nevertheless, he adds, it is quite necessary when
hounds are running to the scent to cheer them on,
so that even a mute hound may speak like Croesus'
son in the story. It is a good thing generally to call
hounds by name. They love to hear their master's
voice, and the knowledge that he has his eye upon
them, and is aware of their gallant behaviour, enlivens
them in all their difficulties. In the first run there

---

[1] προκαλοῦνται τὰς κύνας Arrian, Cyn. 16, I am following the
text very closely—giving it in English in fact with an occasional
comment.   Note the image of war again marked on all this passage
[2] Ch. III above.

is no harm in calling on them as often as you please:
but in the second or third, when hard work is telling
upon them, a call by name should be made sparingly,
because there is risk that a hound may be driven by
his high spirit, his keenness, and his desire to please
his master, to strain beyond his powers and so get
a rupture. Many a first-class hound has come to
grief in that manner. So let them carry on the
contest in their own fashion.[1] Remember that it
is not an even match between hare and hound: the
hare takes a line at her good pleasure, and the hound
has to follow it. The hare, by doubling and twisting,
can throw off the hound and run on ahead, while
the hound flung away from the scent is at fault, and
has to cast about for a fresh line and to recover all
the distance lost. Moreover all rugged country,
with clefts or boulders or steep rises and falls in the
ground, gives the hare a clear advantage; for she
has little weight to carry, and the fur on her feet
saves them from damage in rough travelling. She
knows too that her life is at stake, and so is rendered
unconscious of difficulties.

When the hound has overhauled the hare and
proved victorious in the chase, jump off your horse
and caress him, lavishing praise, stroking his head,
pulling his ears out, and exclaiming, " Well done,
Tawny ! well done, Speedy ! bravo, Ravager !" or
whatever the name of the hound happens to be:
for hounds are just as fond of praise as the best of
human beings:[2] and if the victor is not beaten to
a standstill, he comes up smiling and with a happy,
friendly air of greeting. It is a good sign then if he
takes a roll on the ground, as horses do, for it shows
that he is not overdone, and it is a rest after work.

[1] How completely this wise counsel is borne out by Badminton !
" When hounds are running well, *leave them alone* is best " (p. 80).

[2] From the use of the word γενναιότατοι one would almost
think that Arrian considered love of praise to be a mark of good
breeding in men (Cyn. 18).

So far Arrian, whose account of taking the field
with harriers differs from Xenophon's mainly in
assuming that his follower of the chase is mounted
and that hounds can be relied upon to run down the
hare pretty often in the open, instead of having to
drive her into an ambush of nets. One may repeat
that this change in the style of hunting—and it must
be remembered that the two descriptions are divided
by a space of about five centuries—arose largely
from the introduction of the Celtic or Gaulish
hound, which had a speed previously unknown. The
exact nature of the breed has yet to be determined :
but when one reflects upon the very ancient commu-
nity of race, language, and customs between the Celts
of south-western Britain and the Celts of north-
western Gaul, it seems reasonable to conjecture
that the Celtic harrier had some relation to the
mysterious hound of Britain, which is no less famous
in Greek and Roman hunting lore.

However that may be, it may be worth while to
follow Arrian's story of hunting as practised by this
far-distant people of Gaul. Those among them who
are wealthy and fond of ease, send out markers at
early dawn to likely places to discover any lay of
a hare, and word is sent back when one or more
hares have been marked down. The hunters then
arrive on horseback, hounds are slipped, and the
chase begins. Where no markers are employed,
a company of sportsmen is got together and take the
field on horseback : they move on to likely ground,
and slip the harriers as soon as a hare is started.
But the true craftsmen of the chase sally out on foot
alone with a single mounted man, whose business it
is to follow the hare close along with the hounds.
They form a wide front and advance in line within
signalling distance of each other, and, crossing and
quartering the ground, work over every yard of
likely cover for a hare.   If they have several hounds

on leash, they must all keep their posts in moving;
else when a hare is put up, not a man there would
refrain from slipping his own hound, everyone wild
with desire to see his hound running, or frantically
excited by the shouting: so that the hare would
be pulled down by a mob of hounds without a
struggle, and all thought of sport would vanish from
the scene. There must be *a master of the hunt*,[1]
and he must see to the coupling of the hounds
and order one to be taken up here, another to be
slipped there, and another to be kept on leash.

The Celts use swift coursing hounds along with
their trackers, and while the trackers cast about, men
stand at intervals in places where the hare is most
likely to break away, holding the best of the coursers
in hand and ready to slip them as required. This
line corresponds fairly to Xenophon's line of nets.
But even so the hunt is often thrown out of order and
the hare, be she never so game, is bewildered by
the clamour of hounds, and unless she gets a good
start at the outset to settle her wits, she is struck
silly and is taken very easily. A man, therefore,
with a trusty hound on leash must not slip him while
the hare is flurried, but let her run and double a few
times first —that is if he does not mean to spoil sport.[2]
A leveret must on no account be chased, and the
trackers must be called off, if possible: but they are
hard to stop: for hunger renders them disinclined to
obey, when they are wild to devour the quarry, so
that you can hardly pull them off even by the use of
the stick.

From the above remarks of Arrian it is clear that
he had a very intimate knowledge of Celtic sport.
I may repeat that he belonged to Nicomedia—a very

---

[1] This is very literal—ἄρχοντα χρὴ ἐπιτετάχθαι τῇ Θήρᾳ—and it is
curious to find the office recognised so early (Arrian, Cyn. 20).

[2] Here again the rendering is exact—εἰ μὴ διαφθείραι ἐθέλει τὴν
θέαν.

beautiful town and district in Asia Minor, which three centuries later Diocletian chose for the capital of the Eastern Empire, and so enlarged and embellished that it rivalled in populousness and in magnificence both Rome and Alexandria:[1] I have said too that his Periplus, or Cruise round the Black Sea, and other works prove him to have been a traveller: but it is often surprising to find that his acquaintance with lands and peoples of the Roman world was as detailed as it was wide. Another instance of this may be given, also in connexion with the Celts, in his own words.

Some of the Celts, he writes, keep the custom of making a yearly sacrifice to Artemis, while others make an offering of treasure. For every hare taken they put two obols[2] in the money-box: for a fox a drachma, because he is a crafty brute, given to destruction of hares, and they regard him as a deadly enemy captured: then for a deer they offer four drachmas, because he is a large animal and represents a nobler form of sport. When the season of Artemis' birthday comes round, the money-box is opened, and they buy a victim with the fund, a sheep, or a goat, or maybe a calf, if the money runs to it. The victim being slain and its firstlings offered to the goddess, they hold that day a great revel for men and hounds alike, and they put garlands on the hounds, thus acknowledging that they are the producers of the feast.[3] All this falls in with Caesar's remark that life in Gaul is made up of hunting.

Here I would once again lay stress upon Arrian's spirit of sportsmanship: indeed I would term him the prince of sportsmen of the ancient world, as this

[1] Gibbon, Ch. XIII. Not far away was the Heraeum at Chalcedon, a site chosen by Theodora for her palace, which with its parks and gardens was reputed the most beautiful in the world.

[2] Say 3d.: a drachma may be put at 10d.

[3] Arrian, Cyn. 34, literally rendered, as usual.

further passage may witness. After speaking of the splendid riding of the Libyan nomads in their chases across the desert, he adds:

" This is the proper way of hunting for all who have good horses and good hounds—not with traps or nets or snares or clever devices to outwit the quarry, but by a straight fight in the open.[1] From the point of view of sport, there is no comparison in my opinion: the one method is a kind of plundering or pilfering, the other is a fair trial of strength in war fought to a finish. One set of hunters, like pirates, make sail stealthily against their quarry and then fall upon him: the others, like those seamen of Athens who won the naval battles against the Persians at Artemisium and Salamis and Psyttaleia and off Cyprus, meet their quarry in open battle and conquer."

On the training and breeding of hounds Arrian has some remarks which differ somewhat, though not very materially, from Xenophon. A bitch, he says, may be taken out to the field when eleven months old; even at ten months, if she has a tight build and no sign of slouching,[2] you may take her to some place with a clear view all round and there, releasing a hare, slip the puppy, who will be thrilled by the sight of the hare close in view and will set to work buoyantly. After a while you must slip a fully-trained hound, to save the puppy from too long a strain, which could only end in complete exhaustion: and the hound, coursing and doubling with ease, will take the hare and hand it over to the puppy to worry to death.

When the puppy is ready for the field, first walk him along very rough roads—which is a good

---

[1] ἐκ τοῦ εὐθέος διαγωνιζόμενοι. This passage is from Cyn. 24. 4. Could anyone doubt that the image of war was always present to Arrian's mind?

[2] εἰ εὐπαγὴς τύχοι καὶ μὴ ὑγρομελής—not easy words to render in English.

practice for hardening his feet—and put the man leading him in some place with an all-round view upon your right. If a hare is put up and gets away in view, the hound must not be slipped.[1] This is the advice which Xenophon rightly gives with respect to hounds that are being trained to follow the scent: but if you slip a swift coursing hound which has not viewed the quarry, he is at a loss and gallops about and riots frantically. Moreover if the hare gets clean away from a full-grown hound, the hound is upset, refuses to come back to his leader and disowns his call to heel, but races and rushes about like a madman for nothing but sheer love of running.

Well, the man with the hound on slip must take his stand in a spot such as has been indicated and get under cover wherever he thinks the hare in distress is likely to bend her way. On view of the hare so distressed, he may slip the young hound at close range, but not fronting the quarry: otherwise the hound will rush forward and go straight for the hare, who will double and throw him off easily, so that he is left far behind and can hardly recover the line— just as a warship sailing straight ahead has much work to alter her course, unless most of the oars change action.[2] Wait, therefore, for the hare to pass, and slip your hound from the flank: but as soon as the hare is pulled down, someone must run up quickly before the hound is glutted with blood— not by any means that a sportsman who hunts for the beauty of the chase will think twice about the loss of food for the larder, but because it is a very

---

[1] The text gives οὐχ ὁρῶσαν μὴ ἐφιέναι, but the οὐχ must have crept in by error. It is absurd to say that in training a young hound to follow scent you must not let him go if he has *not* seen the hare: unleashing on view would teach him not to work out the scent, and would be the worst possible lesson.

[2] Some of the oars must easy, some hold water, some back water, and some pull. Sails counted for little in wearing such a vessel.

bad lesson for a well-bred puppy to learn to devour the hare.[1] Moreover that is the way in which many hounds have been destroyed, when panting hard after a long run they gorge till they choke to death. A hound should never by any chance be allowed to follow a fox, as that ruins him for the field completely.

Dog hounds must not be taken out to hunt till they are two years old: because their frames take so much longer to become knit and settled firmly. It is not a small risk to run: for many a hound who enters the lists before he is fully grown dies an early death, and the better the hound is bred, the more likely is he to suffer, because his high spirit keeps him running to the limit of his powers. For the rest, the rules to be observed in training bitches apply equally to dog hounds.

This concludes Arrian's account of hunting with harriers. Certain details in which he differs from Xenophon have already been noted: one may add that the discrepancy between the two writers in regard to the age at which puppies may be taken out for field training is not so real as it might seem. Xenophon gives eight months for bitches and ten months for dog hounds, whereas Arrian gives ten or eleven months for a bitch and two years for a dog: but it is clear that in the practice of Xenophon's day the puppy was kept under much closer control, by means of long leashes or otherwise, and so was saved from some of those dangers to his habits or his physique against which Arrian utters his warning.

---

[1] This passage is worth giving in the original—ἁλόντος δὲ [τοῦ λαγῶ] ἐφομαρτείτω τις σπουδῇ πρὶν ἐμφορηθῆναι τοῦ αἵματος τὴν κύνα, οὐχ ὅτι δὴ τὰ κρέα ἄρα περὶ πολλοῦ ποιητέον ἀνδρὶ ἐς κάλλος κυηγετοῦντι, ἀλλ' ὅτι πονηρὸν μάθημα κυνὶ γενναίᾳ λαγὼ ἐσθίειν (Cyn. 25. 9). Here once more Arrian defines true sportsmanship as the characteristic of a man who hunts for the beauty of the chase—αὐτὸ τὸ ἐν θήρᾳ καλόν—as quoted above in Ch. III.: and that is not only the nearest Arrian gets to the term, but the truest definition for all time.

Moreover Xenophon was always contemplating a
form of hunting in which as a rule runs were
shorter, the object being rather to circumvent the
hare and drive her into an entanglement of nets
carefully arranged beforehand: whereas Arrian was
thinking of a fair field in the open, not beset with
any such barriers or contrivances to diminish the
chances of a long run.   In other words the difference
of opinion with regard to the proper age for young
hounds to hunt depends upon a difference of method,
and a consequent difference in the degree of danger
to the constitution of the harrier puppy.   Risks
which were not felt in the days of short runs and long
leashes had to be taken very seriously five hundred
years later when sport provided long runs—often
without a check.

Nevertheless it would be a mistake to imagine
that the use of nets as an aid to hunting had dis-
appeared by Arrian's time.   True that with harriers
it was regarded as both unnecessary and unsportsmanlike to lay traps of the kind or to hamper the
free course of the hare: and as this opinion prevailed
in the more broken country round Nicomedia where
Arrian lived, it had probably won its way to the rich
plains of Elis, where Xenophon hunted, and to
Oppian's home in Cilicia.   But in the pursuit of
wild beasts of the mountain and forests—a pursuit
in which tactics were as important as open battle—
the use of nets never went out of fashion.

CHAPTER VI

LARGER GAME

Stag—Wild Boar—Lion—Bear—Leopard—Hunting by Music—
Trapping and other Devices—Ethiopians fighting Lions—
Question of Hunting Horn—The Scare of Feathers—Tiger
Cubbing—Other Wild Animals—Story of Bacchus—Hunting
by Wine.

WHILE hare-hunting stood for so much in the
mind of the classic sportsman, other forms
of the chase were neither unknown nor undervalued,
although it may be doubted whether in any one of
them the pure pleasure of hunting—αὐτὸ τὸ ἐν θήρᾳ
καλόν—was so dominant and so uɹalloyed. Look,
for example, at Xenophon's account of stag-hunting.
Indian (or Tibetan) hounds[1] are recommended for
their size, strength, courage, and spirit—qualities
which guarantee endurance: and the young fawns
are to be hunted in spring, the season of their birth.
First move on to meadow-land and look round to
discover where most hinds are gathered. To that
spot the houndsman must go before daybreak with
hounds and javelins: then having tied up the hounds
in covert some way off, to prevent them from viewing
the hinds and giving tongue, he must take up a good
post for watching. As day dawns, the hinds are seen
bringing the fawns to their several resting-places,
and after suckling them as they lie on the ground,
and looking well round to make sure that they are
not observed, they move away, but keep an eye
on their offspring. Thereupon the hounds may be
untied, and the hunter, having carefully marked the

[1] Mr. Marchant alleges with reason that Thibetan dogs are
intended.

77

spot where he saw the nearest fawn, can go forward
with his javelins towards it, remembering that the
near view will differ from the distant view. On
spying the fawn he may approach it and will find
it lying still, as if trying to squeeze into the ground.
The fawn may then be lifted and given to the net-
keeper, but it will make a loud bleating, whereupon
the dam will come running up to the rescue. This is
the moment to launch your javelins and set on the
hounds, and when you have secured your victim,
you can proceed against others, using exactly the
same tactics.

But this kind of hunting is good only with very
young fawns. When they are more grown, they
feed with the others, and if pursued make off in
front or in the middle of the herd, rarely at the rear,
and the hinds trample the hounds in their defence.
Unless therefore a man happens to drop among
them at the start, and scatters them so that one is
cut off from the rest, the hunting is very difficult.
Even then it is a tremendous strain on the hounds
and they are beaten in the first run: for the fawn
at that age has an incredible speed, which is further
quickened by terror. But his frame is not yet
hardened for endurance, and in the second or third
run he is more easily overtaken.

Another way of taking deer was by means of traps
called " foot-twisters," which were set in the high-
lands or in meadows or brooks or glades or farm-
lands or any haunt of the quarry. These traps,
ten or twelve inches high, were formed of basket-
work with a crown or hoop at the top and with an
arrangement of iron and wooden spikes alternating
inside. On the crown of the trap was fixed a noose
with a slip-knot on a stout rope, to which was
fastened a small log of oak. The trap was buried
in a hole of such a depth that the crown came
nearly level with the surface of the ground: the rope

and the oak log were also sunken in a shallow trench.
Loose earth from the hole had to be taken away
some distance: then a layer of twigs was put over
the trap and lightly covered with leaves: on this
some of the surface soil, and then a layer of fresh
clods from a distance, so that the deer shall neither
see the trap nor be aware that the soil has been
disturbed. The hunter took out his hounds to

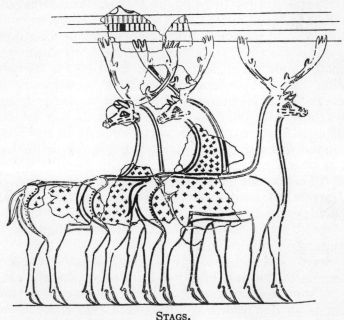

STAGS.
From a fresco at Tiryns, c. 1500 B.C.

make a round of the mountain traps at daybreak or
later, but in the sown lands night was the only time.
When he found a trap broken through, he slipped
his hounds and hallooed them forward along the
trail left by the clog. If the deer had been caught
by the forefoot, he was soon overtaken, as the clog
swinging about hit him all over: and if the hind-
leg was caught, the dragging of the clog sorely

hampered his run, and sometimes the clog got so entangled and wedged among bushes that the deer was brought to a stand. But the hunter in either case had to keep his distance, for a deer brought to bay would fight horn and hoof and must be killed by the throw of a spear.

The deer must have suffered a good deal with his foot caught in a ring of basket-work studded with nails and his leg gripped by a noose and dragging a clog of some weight.[1] Xenophon has no word of disapproval for these unsportsmanlike proceedings, and it is pretty clear that such devices were employed not by sportsmen in love with hunting for its own sake, but by professional hunters or trappers in search of a livelihood. Moreover country holed by these foot-twisters would be as dangerous for riding as the most heavily wired country in any hunt today. Yet the trap remained in use for centuries: it is clearly named in the Greek anthology by Philip of Thessalonica (first century A.D.),[2] in a line of Grattius,[3] and still later Pollux mentions it.[4] Arrian has little about stag-hunting, but he would not have adopted such methods, and all his language is language of a fair chase.

Stags and other large game, he says, require hounds of the best breed to hunt them: for the stag is a huge animal, covers a long distance in a run, and is so dangerous an antagonist that there is no small risk of life for an enterprising hound. Where there are fairly level plains, as in Mysia, the country of the Getae, Scythia, and Illyria, the stag is hunted by men mounted on Scythian or Illyrian horses.

---

[1] It was about 2 ft. 3 ins. long and 3 ins. in diameter. Xenophon elsewhere says that this trap was used for wild-boars also.

[2] Anth. P. VI. 107: νευροπλεκεῖς τε κνωδάλων ἐπισφύρους ὠκεῖς ποδίστρας.

[3] I. 92: Quid si dentatas iligno tobore clausit
    Venator pedicas ?

[4] V. 32. πεδοστράβη is named.

These are slow goers at first, and you would perhaps think mighty little of them compared with horses from Thessaly, or Sicily, or the Peloponnese: but for a hard day's work they can hold out against anything whatever. On such a day you may see a fast, upstanding, proud-looking horse beaten to a standstill, while a lean and mangy cob first catches him up, next passes and shows him his heels, and then rattles the stag along, never giving in until the quarry, utterly spent and bewildered, stands there panting, and you can either spear him at close quarters just as if he were tied up, or, if you prefer it, you can lasso him and take him alive.

Though Oppian has a good deal to say about the natural history and habits of various kinds of deer, stag-hunting does not seem to have been an amusement which he followed, because, as he tells us at the outset, his stories of the chase are generally founded on his own experience, and he is silent on this particular form of sport. We may pass on to boar-hunting, and return to Xenophon, who lived in a country famous in legend for the great size of its boars.[1] He gives nets, spears, javelins, and foot-traps as the main apparatus of the chase, for which Indian, Cretan, Locrian, or Spartan hounds of first-class strain are recommended as good fighters. Pindar too describes the hound of Sparta from Taÿgetus as the cleverest of all four-footed creatures at hunting (Fr. 73): and one may remark here with what force Shakespeare's extraordinary knowledge even of things classical comes home. In Midsummer Night's Dream (IV. 1) he makes Hippolyta say:

I was with Hercules and Cadmus once
When in a wood of Crete they bayed the boar
With hounds of Sparta. Never did I hear
Such gallant chiding. . . .

[1] When Heracles brought home the boar of Erymanthus, King Eurystheus was so scared at the sight of the carcase that he fled and hid himself in a copper cauldron.

6

and Theseus replies:

> My hounds are bred out of the Spartan kind,
> So flewed, so sanded, and their heads are hung
> With ears that sweep away the morning dew;
> Crook-kneed and dewlapped like Thessalian bulls,
> Slow in pursuit, but matched in mouth like bells,
> Each under each. A cry more tunable
> Was never holla'd to, nor cheered with horn,
> In Crete, in Sparta, nor in Thessaly.

The music of hounds was clearly loved as much in Shakespeare's day as in Mr. Jorrocks': but there is nothing quite corresponding to this delight in the melodious chorus of hounds to be found in classical writings. Xenophon goes on to say that stout nets are required, and the rope of the mesh must be woven of three strands, each strand made up of fifteen threads: the top and bottom border ropes must be half as thick again, and be furnished with metal rings to take a running rope.[1] The javelins or hurling spears of every sort must have broad keen blades and strong shafts; the thrusting spears have blades 15 inches long, with strong teeth or prongs welded on the socket, the shaft of cornel wood, as thick as the shaft of a soldier's pike; and a company of several huntsmen must work together. The teeth on the spear-head are up-turned, *i.e.* curved towards the point of the spear—not the butt.

When they reach a place in which they believe the boar to harbour, a single Spartan hound is slipped to cast about, and the other hounds are taken round

---

[1] Xen. Cyn. X. 2. The depth of the net is not clear: Mr. Marchant puts it at about twelve feet. But the nets for large game were made of rope and very strong: those which are shown in painting or sculpture often look like fences of trellis-work. Two or more men were required for carrying even a short length of such netting. The cloud-net for small birds was so called for its lightness in contrast to the heavy rope meshes.

STAG-HUNTING.
1. From the so-called sarcophagus of Alexander the Great.
2. From a Pompeian painting.

To face page 77.

HUNTING THE BOAR OF CALYDON.

From an Attic vase at Berlin.

(Note the graceful figure of Atalanta, the use of leggings, mace, and double axe.)

To face page 83.

on leash[1] with him. As soon as a trail is found, the
hunters follow it in single file and will read their
own signs of the boar's passage in hoof-prints,
broken saplings, or barked trunks of trees. The
trail which the hound follows will usually lead to a
dense covert, in which boars like to harbour, and on
finding the lair the hound will give tongue: the boar,
however, generally refuses to be roused. In that
case call off the hound and tie him up with the rest
of the pack at some distance. Now is the time to
arrange the nets, which must be set in the most
convenient and likely places, and every net should
have a deep salient or pocket, the sides supported on
forked props, care being taken to allow plenty of
light to get through the meshes. The guide rope
running along the bottom of the net must be securely
anchored to the trunk of a tree.

The nets being all duly placed, the company take
their javelins and hunting spears, untie all the hounds,
and go forward in wide open order,[2] so that the boar
may have a clear passage, if he wheels about and
declines to be driven forward: otherwise, if the line
is too close, someone is likely to be damaged when he
charges back. The most practised huntsman goes
ahead of the line with the hounds, hallooing them
forward till they reach the boar's lair and make for
him. Rising up in alarm, he will toss any hound
that meets him in front, and will charge up to the
nets. Finding his way barred, he will stand still,

---

[1] Shakespeare also thought of the boar-hounds as taken to the
hunting ground on leash. A few lines before the passage quoted
in the text above, Theseus remarks:

> My love shall hear the music of my hounds
> Uncoupled in the western valley.

[2] ἀπολείποντας ἀπ' ἀλλήλων πολὺ in the Greek. The whole
context, and indeed the very nature of the case, requires the interpretation I have given, as against Mr. Marchant's " keeping well
behind one another," which would imply an advance in line ahead.
Such a line would be useless for driving the boar towards the nets:
it must be line abreast which is intended.

and this is the moment for the hounds to press hard
upon him, while the hunters hurl stones and javelins
from a distance to make him shove against the mesh
hard enough to pull the guide-rope tight and so close
the net.   Then the most expert and most powerful
man in the field may come up in front and drive his
spear into him.

If, however, in spite of the shower of stones and
javelins he fails to shove into the net, but wheels
about to the rear and makes for one of his assailants,
that man must advance with his spear couched, his
legs as in wrestling not far apart, left foot forward
and left hand foremost on the shaft.   The boar's
eye and every movement of his head must be keenly
watched, or by a sudden jerk of his tusks he may
knock the spear out of the hunter's hand.   In that
case the man should fall flat on his face and cling hard
to the underwood, because in that position the boar
with his upcurved tusks cannot get a lift on him,
whereas in a raised posture he is certain to be gored
and battered.   Failing to raise his enemy, the boar
stands over and tramples him: and then the only
chance of escape from such deadly peril is for one of
his fellow-huntsmen to rush up with his spear
balanced for throwing, though he dare not cast it
for fear of killing his comrade: but as the boar will
turn in a frenzy of rage on the newcomer, the man
on the ground can jump up, recover his spear, and
with the same grip must drive it into the boar's
chest inside the shoulder-blade.   Such is the force
of a charging boar, that but for the metal prongs
on the socket of the spear the shaft would drive
home far enough to bring the boar's tusks close to
the man.   By the metal prongs may possibly be
meant cross-pieces rather than short spikes: in any
case the points are curved upwards towards the point
of the spear.   It is somewhat strange that Xenophon
makes no mention here of the hunting-knife, which

surely the hunter carried, and which would have
stood him in good stead when overthrown by the
boar. Martial has two lines upon the hunting-
knife founded on this very incident:

> Si dejecta gemes longo venabula rostro,
> Hic brevis in grandem cominus ibit aprum;

i.e., if you groan as the boar's long snout wrenches
the spear from your grasp, you can plunge the short
knife into his carcase at close quarters.[1]

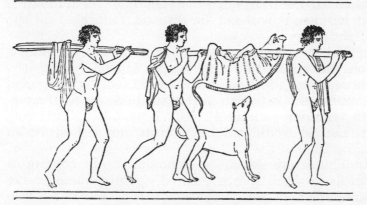

BRINGING HOME THE BOAR.
From a Greek vase painting.

The same practice of couching the spear and
standing left foot foremost to receive the charge of a
lion is commended by Oppian.[2]

There is another way of going after boar. Nets
are set in paths leading up from the vales to oak
copses, in winding glens, rocky places, or in runs
down to marsh-land or pools of water. At every net
a hunter is posted, and when the hounds have found

[1] Ep. XIV. 31. So Tac. Ann. III. 43 couples spear and knife
for hunting.
[2] Cyn. II. 475-8

their quarry and driven him into a net, the hunter
must finish him with his spear. In very hot weather
the boar may even be run down by hounds, for in
spite of his enormous strength he tires out after
prolonged hard breathing. Many hounds are killed
in this kind of hunting, and the men too run danger
of their lives: for when the boar is at bay, standing
in water or on a steep slope or in covert, the hunter
advancing with his spear is certain to be charged.
Nevertheless advance he must and show in action
the spirit which determined his love of the sport.
Spear at the charge, and left shoulder forward: then
if he falls, it will not be through failure to do the
right thing.

Yet it is curious that in the lion hunt sculptured
on the relief from the tombs of the Nasos[1] the
hunters are shown with their *right* foot foremost and
spears held on the left side of the body for encounter-
ing the lion—surely an artist's mistake. That way
the stand would not be so firm, nor the thrust so
powerful.

This lively sketch of Xenophon's—in colours as
fresh as when it was painted—brings home to the
sportsman of today the manner of the chase two
thousand four hundred years ago, with the laws of
its craft and its scenes of excitement and danger.
Nor can anyone who, like the present writer, has
taken part in a boar hunt in the Ardennes, fail to
remark many points of analogy as well as difference.
Hunters nowadays are armed with smooth-bore or
rifle instead of spear,[2] but carry a good knife for use
at close quarters. The guns are posted some forty
yards apart in a long line, and wait in dead silence
for the game to be driven towards them. A company

[1] Bellori II. Tav. XXVII.
[2] The spear, of course, is used in pig-sticking in India, and
a boar hunt there on horseback is very much the same as that in
which the Emperor Trajan is depicted as distinguishing himself.

of beaters with hounds has started a mile or two away
in the forest: they, too, are ranged in line, with flank
guards slightly in advance, and slowly they drive
the covert towards the guns. A very faint winding
of a horn in the far distance is the first warning to the
guns to stand on the alert. The sound grows more
frequent and becomes louder, till one can hear the
hounds baying and the men shouting and the boars—
sometimes several together—come crashing through
the thicket, but often unseen till they are close in
front of the guns. The boar, as often as not, will
stand a few seconds in surprise at seeing a man in
front, and that is the moment for a quick and steady
aim to bring him down. To miss or to wound is
certain danger. But at times the boar refuses to
face the guns, and I have seen four or five of them
together worried with hounds and terriers at their
heels as they turned away, while beaters and hounds
were so close to the guns that to get a shot was
impossible.

There was, however, a much more polite way of
hunting the fierce and unmannerly boar, according
to AElian.[1] He recalls a Tyrrhenian (or Etruscan)
story that wild boars and stags in that country are
captured not merely with nets and hounds—the
usual form of hunting and no doubt a rough business
—but by the gentle aid of music. There is the ring
of nets and other usual accessories: but an accomplished flute-player takes his stand, softening his
notes, avoiding all stress, and piping the sweetest
and most harmonious melodies. A great calm
spreads in the forest, as the strains float over mountain
and glen and thicket, reaching all the holds and
harbours of the wild beasts. They at first are
startled and alarmed: then unmixed and uncontrolled

---

[1] AEl. XII. 46. He is here in one of his poetic moods and
may exaggerate this story, in which music so far soothes the savage
breast as to lure boars to destruction.

delight in the music steals upon them, so that under
the charm they forget their young and their home—
a thing much against their wont. They are thus
drawn on slowly as under a spell, till by the enchantment of the strain they come forth and fall into the
nets, overmastered by music. Surely in all this the
legend of Orpheus was a living force.

The poems of Oppian are disappointing in the
scantiness of their allusions to hunting the wild
boar. There is no description of such a chase: but
that it was known to him, and that it existed in a
form more like Indian pig-sticking, may be gathered
from a single line,[1] in which he says that the horse
required for boar hunting is one with a fiery, flashing
eye, as this denotes high spirit and courage. On
the other hand he lays stress on a point scarcely
noticed by Xenophon, when he urges that in hunting
with nets, and indeed in all hunting, the game
should be tracked and driven *up wind*, because all
wild animals have a very keen sense of smell, and
if they wind man or dog they will rush away, even
turning on their pursuers to escape. This rule
of the wind must be kept most carefully even in
arranging the positions of the nets and setting them.
Any movement down wind may ruin the day's sport.

Lions and bears, leopards, lynxes, and panthers
are briefly referred to by Xenophon as found in
mountain ranges in countries abroad, such as Mount
Pangaeus and Cittus beyond Macedonia, in Mysian
Olympus and Pindus, or in Nysa beyond Syria.
In some places where the ground was impossible for
hunting, aconite poison, mixed with some favourite
food of the wild beast, is put about their watering-
places or other haunts. Another plan, and a very
dangerous one, is for armed and mounted men to cut
them off when they go down to the plain at night and
intercept their return. Yet another is to trap them

[1] Cyn. I. 309.

in a deep pit.   A large round cavity is dug out leaving
a column of earth in the middle.   Towards evening
a goat is brought and tied up on this column, and the
whole pit is surrounded with a thick hedge of brushwood without any opening.   The wild beasts hearing
the goat bleating come up and run round and round
the enclosure, looking in vain for an entrance, then

GENERAL HUNTING SCENE.

leap over the barrier, and tumble down into the pit,
where they are captured or slain.

The places named by Xenophon for the prevalence
of lions and other large animals in his time are worth
noting.   Mount Pangaeus was near the sources of
the river Nestus in what is now the Balkan range,
and it was there, according to the legend, that Orpheus
played on the lyre while all the mountains listened,

the rivers stood still, and the wild beasts of the forest were lulled by the enchantment of his melodies. Mount Cittus was in the same region, while Pindus, the haunt of the Muses, was in the chain of mountains some way to the south-east, near where Thessaly, Epirus, and Macedonia meet: and that is the most southerly point at which lions were known in Greece, although they lingered on in Thessaly until about the first century of our era. Nysa is vaguely described as beyond Syria and authorities have differed about its position. But in Xenophon's time the term Syria denoted a far larger region than today. Herodotus distinctly says that " Syria borders on Egypt,"[1] and the term *beyond Syria* seems to point to Northern Arabia. In Vergil Mount Nysa is made the haunt of tigers, and it was there that Bacchus found and tamed the team of tigers that drew his chariot.[2] Mysia was the country bordering the Dardanelles on the east and was well known to Xenophon, who came there after the Retreat of the Ten Thousand. But it is curious that he defines no other localities in Asia Minor as lion-haunted, omitting even Lycia, which lies towards the south-east of Asia Minor, and is one of the districts in which lions survived the longest. For Sir Charles Fellows, in offering an ingenious explanation of Hesiod's Chimaera with its three heads (lion, goat, and serpent), says of Lycia—" Lions still live in the mountains, the goat is found at the top, while the serpent infests the base of the Cragus."[3] This was in the middle of the nineteenth century.

Oppian, who dwelt in Cilicia, knew a good deal about lions, though he does not definitely make them denizens of Asia Minor. The oryx, which he names as fearlessly lowering its horns when

---

[1] Hdt. II. 116: ὁμουρέει γὰρ ἡ Συρίη Αἰγύπτῳ.
[2] AEn. VI. 806: Liber agens celso Nysae de vertice tigres.
[3] Travels in Asia Minor, p. 348 (1852).

ORPHEUS.
From a Pompeian painting.

To face page 87.

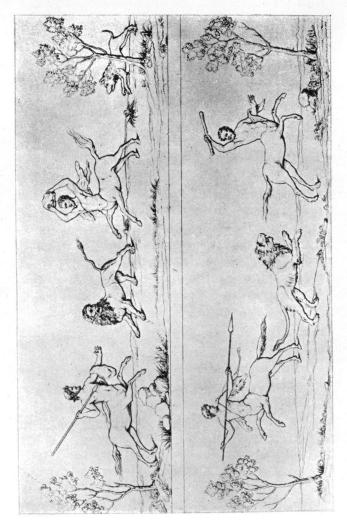

CENTAURS LION-HUNTING.
From a Pompeian painting.

To face page 91.

menaced by a lion, dwelt in the deserts of Syria and
Arabia. Lions of Armenia and Parthia he names.
Those of Arabia Felix are a most eminently handsome
breed, though a rare one: while the Libyans are
the mightiest and are kings of all king lions of the
world. There was a rare black lion from Ethiopia,[1]
found on one occasion in Libya, which caused great
astonishment: and this animal the poet not merely
heard of but saw, when it was brought over for some
royal spectacle. He describes a pitfall similar to
the one mentioned by Xenophon in rather more
detail. First the lion's den is discovered, a mountain
cave from which he issued to seize on cattle and
terrify the herdsmen; and men mark the well-worn
track leading down to his watering-place. Near it
they dig a great deep pit, round in form, and in the
middle of it they build a large and lofty stone column[2]
on the top of which a newly-weaned lamb is tethered.
Outside near the edge of the pit a wall of loose stones,
but closely set, is built high enough to screen the
pit from view. The bleating of the lamb is heard
by a lion, who comes prowling all round the wall,
lashing his tail and flashing his eyes as he finds no
opening. So raging, he springs over the barrier,
and lands much to his astonishment at the bottom
of the pit. Then the hunters, who have kept their
watch unseen some way off, come forward; and
finding the lion rushing and rioting about in the trap
from which there is no escape, they lower a strong
and finely constructed cage hung upon long belts of
leather. Inside the cage is a piece of roasted meat;

---

[1] Ethiopia is a term of ill-defined meaning. Prof. Mair says that
the Ethiopians of Oppian are those on the east of the Persian
Gulf in the region of Baluchistan. In the Odyssey, I. 22-25, it
must refer to African tribes: so in Lucan, Phars. IX. 651, and
so it must be here.

[2] This is proved by Oppian, who says that for jackals and
leopards a much smaller pit was used with a pillar of hewn oak
instead of hewn stone (Cyn. IV 214-5).

and when the lion enters and seizes the bait, a sliding
door closes upon him, and they haul him out from
his prison.

But here the light fails, just as curiosity becomes
wide awake. That this pitfall business was practised
in Libya, Oppian tells us: that its purpose was to
capture the lion alive, is beyond doubt: but how the
cage was got up from the deep hole to the level
ground is left a mystery. It stands to reason that the
cage was a marvel of clever construction: but when
one remembers the size of a fine African lion, one must
own that the cage required to contain him would have
to measure not less than 7 ft. by 5 ft. by 5 ft. A
heavy wooden cage of these dimensions, strong
enough for safety, would weigh several hundred-
weight even when empty, and, with the ponderous
bulk and bones of a full-grown lion added, would
require such a power of resistance in the leathern
belts by which the cage was lowered, and such a force
of human muscle in lifting the weight, as cannot
well be imagined. There is only one solution of the
resulting problem. The pit must have been at
least 10 ft. deep and 20 ft. in diameter. Apart from
the question of weight, no two points on the circum-
ference of the pit could have been chosen (if regard
is had to the column in the centre) to give both
a sure foothold for two parties of men hauling
and direct leverage for raising the cage. It follows
that the plan must have been to break down and fill
in one side of the pit, and so gradually to build a
ramp sloping down to the cage: then, when the
surface of the ramp had been sufficiently trodden
down or pounded to harden it, the cage could be
dragged up on rollers by a comparatively moderate
number of men hauling at the leather belts, on which
there would be no breaking strain, or by a windlass.
Yet that was not the end. The hunters and their
prey had a long and laborious journey over the

desert to some harbour on the coast, where the lion
was shipped across the Mediterranean. The system
of transport must have been marvellously efficient
and have worked with a smoothness hardly to be
surpassed today.

A different kind of pitfall—probably covered with
brushwood—was used sometimes for leopards. The
bait was a dog hung aloft by a cord tightened round
his loins, so that he howled and yelped in pain.

Lion Hunt with Net and Shields.

His cries resounding through the forest soon attracted
a leopard, who came up and took a running leap at
his ready prey. But, by some mechanical device,
the spring of the leopard released a weight attached
to the hanging cord, and the dog was swung up—
doubtless on a pulley—out of reach of the leopard,
who fell down into the pit. Oppian remarks upon
the hunter's callous cruelty to his dog in a tone of
mild poetic disapproval.[1]

[1] Hal. III. 386 *seq.* The story comes as a simile in a fishing tale.

Lions and other wild beasts were taken alive for
the *venationes*, or hunting shows, at which they were
exhibited and made to massacre each other, or to
fight with men,[1] at Rome, and the number of such
animals produced for a single day's entertainment
is incredible. Scaevola was the first to stage a battle
of lions: Sulla showed one hundred at a time: Pompey
six hundred, of which three hundred and fifteen were
males: and Caesar four hundred.[2] Pater has left
a splendid description of such an exhibition at
Ephesus in Marius the Epicurean (Ch. XIV.) and a
vivid analysis of the emotions it stirred.

Lions are mentioned in Homer as attacked or
driven off[3] when plundering cattle-folds, but not as
hunted for sport: although there can be no question
that from very ancient times lion-hunting was so
regarded in Hellas. The famous dagger of Mycenae,
for example, has a hunting scene in which three lions
are being attacked by men armed with bows and
spears. Homer also cites lions and wild boars as
models of strength.[4] So in Hesiod one of the
scenes on the Shield of Heracles is a battle between
lions and boars.[5] But in both poets, while the boar
is spoken of as lawful game for the chase, the lion is
regarded rather as a dangerous beast of prey only
to be encountered in defence of one's own life or
property. But this idea was greatly modified at
a later date, when, as under the Roman Empire,
lion-hunting definitely took its rank as a sport and
even as an exclusively royal sport in certain regions.
Thus on the Arch of Constantine at Rome there is
a medallion showing the Emperor Hadrian with
a lion at his feet, and up to the year A.D. 414 it is

[1] Martial, De Spect. 6, speaks of a woman fighting a lion in the
amphitheatre.
[2] Plin. N.H. VIII. 20.
[3] Il. XVIII. 579 *seq.* Shield of Achilles.
[4] Il. V. 782.
[5] Asp. 148 *seq.*

said that lion-hunting was reserved for the emperors.[1]
But the task of providing lions for the great spectacles
in Rome cannot have been hampered by any such
edict, which must have been merely local.

Oppian mentions what appears to be a chance
encounter in a simile, when he compares the oryx
lowering its horns against the attack of a powerful
wild animal, to a valiant hunter, highly skilled in
his craft, who is charged by a savage lion in the
forest and stands with his feet well set apart and
his spear well couched to receive him.[2] The same
writer depicts another hunting scene in Asia—on
the banks of the Euphrates[3]—in which the lion is
driven into a large crescent-shaped net, carefully
set and closely staked. Three men lie in ambush,
one at the middle and one at each horn of the
crescent. Of the hunters some are mounted on
horses of high courage, others are on foot, carrying
blazing pinewood torches in their right hand and
a metal shield in their left. When the lions are
found, the horsemen charge and the men on foot
follow, waving their torches and clanging their shields
with a furious din, which makes the beasts turn,
gnashing their teeth in rage, but refusing to fight.[4]
So the hunt advances in disciplined order, and the
lions are driven into the crescent of the net, which
is then closed at the ends about them.

But the boldest of all methods of hunting the lion
was practised by the Ethiopians, and consisted in
a series of close personal encounters by a company
of hunters very lightly armed, but working together.
They covered their entire bodies with sheepskins,
well-fitted and hung on straps, as a defence against
the lion's claws: helmets or caps also protected their
heads: they carried large round shields, made of

---

[1] Cod. Theodos. XV. 11. 1.   [2] Cyn. II. 474-8.
[3] The reference is to Armenia and Parthia: see ib. I. 276-7
[4] Ib. IV. 112-139.

plaited osiers and overlaid with strong bull-hide: and for weapons they seem to have had nothing but bows and arrows. As they go forward towards the lion's den, they challenge him with a loud cracking of whips, whereupon he leaps out roaring and flashing his eyes like the lightning, and raging in wrath that rings to the clouds. Rushing on one of the hunters he seizes and begins to maul him, but another hunter runs nimbly behind the lion, shouting and dinning and shooting arrows into him, till he drops his first victim and sweeps round on his new assailant. That is the time for others to attack him on the flank or again on the rear, and so harassed on all sides and bewildered by this changing warfare, seizing one man here, there dashing another to the ground or breaking his neck, at length worn out by wounds and loss of blood he falls, like some mighty warrior, encircled by a ring of foemen in battle, who sweeps his sword round his head now this way and now that, till his strength fails and he sinks to the ground.[1]

With this compare Pliny's testimony, as follows: The noble bearing of the lion is most marked in time of danger. He despises the hunters' weapons at first, defending himself only by the terror of his glance, and as it were protesting that he acts only on compulsion: he is roused more by wrath at the madness of his assailants than by sense of his own peril. His lofty spirit is strongly manifest: when pressed by a great company of hunters and hounds he retires slowly in scorn, stopping from time to time, in open country where he can be plainly seen, but on passing into thicket or forest, he bounds along at great speed, as if he felt that the shame of his flight was hidden in those surroundings. His quick eye picks out in a moment a man who has wounded him, however large the crowd: if a man throws

[1] Id. Cyn. IV. 147-211.

a spear and misses, the lion seizes him, gives him
a shaking, and lays him on the ground without
hurting him. The lion does battle for his whelps:
but he is void of low cunning, looks his enemy in
the face, and hates to be looked at with eyes aslant.[1]

Well, then, may the Greek poet sing of his admiration for the pluck of these wild Ethiopian hunters.
But the courage of the lion moves him no less, and
elsewhere he describes a lioness standing over her
cubs, roaring defiance against the hunters, reckless
of the spears and slings and arrows that pierce her,
torn all over with wounds, yet undaunted in fierce
valour, and fighting on to the death.[2]

Bears have scarcely any notice bestowed upon
them in Xenophon's Treatise on Hunting: but
no one in the ancient world had a good word for
them. Oppian speaks of " cold-blooded bears with
their baleful courage,"[3] and calls them " a murderous,
crafty-witted race, with a shaggy coat of fur, ugly
shape, a mien unchangeably sullen, a villainous
mouth set with sharp teeth, dark snout and keen
shifty eyes, paws like human hands or feet: they are
nimble and turn swiftly: their roar is terrible, their
cunning deep, their heart ferocious."[4] It is clear
that in words like these there is not a trace of the
sympathy and admiration bestowed on the majestic
mien, fine nature, and gallant fighting of the lion.[5]
Nor was the bear hunted with the same show of
honour. The common practice was to discover his
retreat, whether in the thick of a forest or in a cave
of the rocks, and to plant netting all round his lair
cutting off all way of escape. Curiously enough
Ovid agrees with the Greek poet in regard to these
larger animals of the chase. The lion, he says,

[1] N.H. VIII. 19. [2] Oppian, Hal. I. 709-718.
[3] Id. Cyn. II. 466. [4] Id. Cyn. III. 139 *seq.*
[5] Pliny, N.H. VIII. 19 gives the lion a character which can only
be expressed by one word in English—chivalrous. His remarks
come just before the passage quoted in the text.

advances dauntless to overthrow the company of
hunters and flings himself against their spears.
Bold beyond measure, he charges, fired with fierce
disdain, his huge muscles quivering, his strength
waxing in wrath. The ungainly bear rolls out of
his cavern in the hills, with nothing but dead weight
and a dull ferocious heart. The boar sets up his
bristles to show his rage, does battle by charging
against the weapons that front him, and dies on
a spear hurled through his heart.[1] If one may
venture the comparison, the lion was regarded as
a grand and glorious warrior, and the boar as a fierce
and lumbering, yet bold, antagonist, while the bear
was looked upon as a cunning, truculent, and malig-
nant savage.

Yet perhaps this prejudice against the bear arose
mainly in countries where he was least known—as
happens to the human race—and so does him some
injustice. A more kindly view is taken by the
charming winged boy in the illustration, who is
slipping his hound at a naughty bear for stealing
his apple. Moreover the bear furnished exciting
sport in countries where he was regularly hunted,
such as Armenia and the mountain ranges north of
the Tigris—regions not very remote on the eastern
side from Cilicia, the home of Oppian. Now
Oppian has left a sketch of a bear hunt, which is
remarkable not only because it is well drawn and well
tinted, but also because it brings out one or two
novel features, which have not been thrown into the
light in scenes of hunting hitherto here recorded.[2]
And it is worth remembering that at the outset of
this very fourth book of The Chase, in which the
bear hunt is depicted, Oppian remarks: " I shall
tell what I have seen with my own eyes, when roaming
through forest in the chase—that glorious giver of
bounties—as well as what I have learnt from men

---

[1] Ovid, Halieutica, 53 *seq.*　　　　　[2] Cyn. IV. 354 *seq.*

BEAR AND APPLE.

From a Pompeian painting.

M·IVLIVS·VICTOR·EX·COLLEGIO

LITICINVM·CORNICINVM

ROMAN HORNS.

Tomb of Julius Victor.

To face page 98.

who have their calling in the chequered mysteries
of this many-sided, delightful art." And, considering the graphic detail with which he renders this
particular scene, one cannot be far wrong in thinking
that it must have passed before his eyes.

The story runs in prose as follows. A large
company of men enter the depths of the forest,
leading hounds on leash, to search for tracks of
a bear. As soon as a trail is found, hounds follow
it, nose to the ground,[1] and all move on with them.
It is a cold scent at first and disappointing: but
ere long a fresher trail is discovered, and with a
bound the hounds leap forward, straining on the
leash, whimpering,[2] and wild with joy. One is
tempted here to insert, as Oppian does, a picture
pretty enough, though not very much to the point,
and out of tune with the storm of the chase.
" As when a maiden in the burst of springtime
wanders over the hills looking for flowers, and the
balmy scent of the violet is wafted from afar on the
breeze, warmth and laughter gladden her heart:
unstintedly she gathers the blooms, and, wreathing
her head about, goes singing back to her home in
the fields "—even so does the bold heart of the
hound rejoice when he winds the bear !

If the comparison could be dropped, the same
picture might be drawn of a country girl in England
rambling across the downs in search of spring
flowers, and it is in such a picture that once more
the old world and the new are seen as one.

However, the story proceeds to say that the
hunter who has come upon the scent holds back the
hound tight on the leash for all his plunging forward,
and returns merrily to the rest of the company to

[1] In the original, *long nose* : which shows that the hounds
had a long pointed head, as one would expect.

[2] The Greek has exactly the same expression—οἰκτρὰ μάλ'
ὑλακόων, which is not well rendered in the Loeb edition by *pitifully
barking*—a term unknown to English sport.

point out the thicket in which he and his fellow have
marked down the bear.   Now comes the turn of
the netsmen, who steal ahead and set the nets in a
curve with a long wing projecting at either end.
The nets are supported by strong stakes: one man
is stationed outside in the middle and one at the
end of each wing, but they have to lie hidden under
piles of brushwood.   The left side of the net is
prolonged by a stout cord, carried on props at a
level of about four feet from the ground: from the
cord all along are hung streamers of various colours:
and feathers of large birds, such as swans or storks
or vultures, are tied to the ends of the ribbons to
flutter and scare the quarry.

A different arrangement is made opposite to the
string of feathers on the right flank of the net,
where the line is prolonged by hiding-places or
posts of ambush, *i.e.* a series of shelters among
rocks, or rude huts made of boughs hastily thrown
together.   In each of these shelters four men crouch,
completely screened from view.   The bear is not
required to take any notice of these rather elaborate
preparations, nor apparently is he so minded.   But
when the signal passes that all is ready and in order,
a mighty blast of the horn rings through the forest.
At this the bear leaping up rushes out with a growl,
looking round angrily.   Up spring the hunters and
advance " in massed battalions "[1] on two sides
blocking the way and driving the beast before them.
Alarmed by the sight and the din, the bear makes
for the open plain seen afar; but another party of
men from ambush cut him off and by shouting
and clanging push him on towards the net and the
feathers, which wave wildly and clatter in the wind.
Utterly moithered and bewildered by the rush of
men from ambush, the shouting, the roar of the

[1] φαλαγγηδὸν κλονέοντες.   This bear hunt is from Oppian,
Cyn. IV. 354-424.

wind, the din of the horn, the scare of the streamers, the bear makes for the net. When once he has entered the pocket, the watchers at the two ends jump out of concealment and with utmost speed draw the guide-rope tight to close the opening, and wind the net round and round the captive beast, keeping clear of his paws, and in the end stifling his rage. This, however, is only done if a powerful man among the hunters manages to slip a noose round one of the forepaws and binds it up tightly either to another leg or to the neck of the bear. If he fails in this somewhat hazardous proceeding, the bear usually tears his way through and escapes: if he succeeds, the bear is skilfully trussed with poles and ropes, and then put in a cage made of oak and pine, and carried off alive. But he fights madly, tooth and claw, and it requires extraordinary adroitness as well as courage to tie him up instead of killing him.

The chief points to notice in this story are first, that here, as in the African lion hunt, the aim was not to kill but to capture. There can be no doubt that as the lion from Libya was sent for a wild-beast show to Rome, so the bear here was sent to some nearer town of the Empire, perhaps to Ephesus, where St. Paul had to fight in the arena.

Next, the horn, which has not hitherto figured in hunting lore, is here mentioned twice over. In the one line it is called a trumpet, σάλπιγξ, in the other a flute, αὐλός, but neither word can be taken literally. It is once more the image of war that suggests to the poet a war trumpet: and not only would the gentle shepherd's pipe be a queer instrument to use in the mellay of a bear hunt, but the term αὐλὸς Ἐνυαλίου, or pipe of war, actually occurs in the Greek Anthology.[1] There can therefore be no doubt that something in the nature of a hunting

[1] Anth. P. VI. 151.

horn was intended, although, as the Greek κέρας
for horn is not known either in the sporting or in
the military sense, one may fairly argue that the
hunting horn was of metal, and so not unlike that
used with hounds today, but much larger.[1] The
curved horn depicted on monuments is nearly
circular: it was slung under the arm of the rider,
with the mouthpiece near his lips, and round his
back over the shoulder, so that the bell-mouth of
the horn sounded in front of him. That it was in
this case a large instrument is implied by Oppian's
verse which makes the blast of the horn πελώριον—
gigantic. No doubt it resembled the French horn
of today. But as it would be quite unreasonable
to say that in classic times the horn was not used
except for bear-hunting in Armenia: so one may
decide that the omission of its mention in other
stories of the chase is accidental. Once again con-
firmation comes from Varro, who says that the
herdsman on a farm must accustom his cattle to do
everything—to come home, to go to pasture, to
feed—*ad bucinam*—to the sound of the horn. This
implies so constant and familiar use of the horn as a
signal to domestic animals, that one may well believe,
even in default of direct and specific evidence, that
the sound of the horn was used to rally and cheer
on hounds, as well as hunters.[2] Illustrations from

[1] This opinion is thoroughly borne out by Varro (L.L. 5. 24-33),
who, writing two hundred years before Oppian, says that horns
(*cornua*) were so called because they were originally made of
ox-horn, whereas now they are *ex aere*, *i.e.* of copper or brass.
So Ovid (Met. I. 98) contrasts the *tuba directi*, or straight trumpet,
with *aeris cornua flexi*, or curving horn of metal. The *tibia*, which
corresponds to the Greek αὐλός, was also a straight wind instrument: yet in another passage Ovid (Met. III. 533) speaks of
adunco tibia cornu—a curious parallel to Oppian's use of αὐλός for
a horn. Vergil also uses the term *aerea cornua* (AEn. VII. 15).
The truth is the rigid terms of prose became elastic in the hands
of the poet.

[2] Varro, R.R. II. 4. 20: and ib. 16. 2. 3. 13 apros ad bucinam
conciere.

the Column of Trajan and the Arch of Constantine show both the curling horn and the straight trumpet: but a smaller horn may have been used for the chase, as it must have been for cattle. For this indeed there is definite evidence. A Herculaneum painting shows a small shrine or temple on four columns and in the centre under the roof is hanging a small curved bugle horn—very possibly dedicated by some hunter.[1]

Next, we must here note the use of the string of feathers and streamers as a scare for turning game in some required direction. Allusions to this device are common enough in Latin literature: indeed the word *formido*, or scare, is used as a technical sporting term, just as much as *bullfinch*, for example, in English. This technical use of the word is most clearly established by Seneca,[2] and the line of Vergil, in which a hunted stag is described as

puniceae saeptum formidine pennae,

will occur to every classical scholar. Here it is clear that scarlet feathers were used: Seneca too speaks of " picta rubenti linea penna," and no doubt that colour would be very effective: whereas in Oppian the feathers are mainly white, although the streamers were of many hues. Vulture feathers had no bright tints, but added to the scare by their repellent odour, it was thought. At any rate this device was in common use all over the Greek and Roman world: nor was the line of waving feathers merely drawn across some section of the hunting ground to form a barrier: it was sometimes set all

[1] Figured in Pitture Antiche d' Ercolano e Contorni, tom. III. p. 309 (Nap. 1790).

[2] De Ira, II. 11-5, quoted by Prof. Mair in his Oppian, p. 192, where a valuable list of references is given: see also his note on the feathers, p. 193 *n.* The line from Vergil is AEn. XII. 750. One may add Grattius, Cyn. 1. 75 *seq.*, and Nemesianus, 1. 304 *seq.*

round a covert where deer were known to harbour,
and when the enclosure was complete the hunters
entered and made an easy prey, as the deer, with
every avenue of escape blocked against them, rushed
about bewildered within the wood.

Tigers were well known in Roman shows, though
they were unheard of before Alexander's conquests
in Asia. They may quite possibly have been
trapped by pitfalls, as lions were, although there is
no definite warrant for that opinion, and it is more
likely that they were stolen as cubs from their
mother. They came from Hyreania and India,
where, as Pliny says,[1] the method of capture was as
follows. A party of hunters went by boat to a
district haunted by tigers, and among them was a
scout who, having discovered a place where a tigress
lodged with a large litter of cubs, lay in ambush
waiting for the mother to leave them. When she
had gone, the hunter came out, and packing the cubs
into a sack or basket made off as fast as he could
to rejoin his comrades. If the tigress came back to
discover her loss, she pursued the robber with a
savage roar at a speed incredible. Having no defence, he threw down one of the cubs, which she
picked up and carried home, where she laid it down,
and returned raging to the chase. So the game
went on, a cub being dropped at every fresh onset
of the tigress, until the robber reached his companions in the boat and, running up the gangway,
pushed off, while the tigress was left plunging and
ramping in baffled fury on the bank.

It might prove an interesting experiment in these
days to see if a tigress who had been robbed of her
cubs, and had discovered and pursued the robber,
would be so far satisfied with the return of her family
by instalments as to keep her claws off him: but some
nerve would be required for the adventure.

[1] N.H. VIII. 25.

TIGER CUBBING.
From a Roman relief.

To face page 105.

This particular scene, however, appears to have been represented by a Roman artist on a marble relief found among the tombs of the Nasos. It is tolerably certain that the sculptor had read the story in Pliny and that he was never present at such a raid on a tigress: so that he cannot be depended on for the details, which were probably bodied forth by his imagination. He depicts a punt-like boat connected by an open gangway with a shore upon which several horsemen are engaging or flying before tigers, and one huntsman is hastily passing a small cub to another, who gallops towards the gangway. Pliny says nothing about mounted men, but it is very unlikely that the plan for stealing the cubs could have been carried out on foot. Large oval shields are nearly always borne by the hunters in the scenes depicted on these monuments—here for example and in the lion hunt described above—and one would like to know whether metal shields were normally part of a hunter's equipment for big game among the Romans. There is some literary evidence to confirm the use, and the Ethiopian custom as recorded by Oppian proves the use of wicker shields among that people.

In the same poet's remarks on the tiger there may be found a somewhat different story. His admiration for the tiger and its marvellous refinement of form and colouring is unbounded. As the peacock surpasses all birds of the air, so does the tiger surpass all beasts of the field in brilliant beauty. The dark stripes which chequer the radiant sheen of his skin; the flashing eyes, frowning brows, and gleaming teeth; the long lithe body and limbs moulded to give incomparable swiftness—all these unite to make the tiger the most glorious animal in the world. Yet he takes no thought of his mate when there is a litter of cubs, but flees before the hunters; while the tigress reft of her cubs follows

them, sorely troubled at heart, and cheers the
hunters mightily *by making straight for their nets*.[1]
Here is quite a new element: and it is clear that,
in Oppian's mind, an ambush of nets played a part
in the game of cub-lifting. This fact makes the
process more intelligible, reduces the danger, and
proves that the aim of the hunters was not merely
to carry off the cubs, but to kill or capture the tigress.
But quite generally the same writer remarks elsewhere[2]
that mounted men are wanted for tiger-hunting.

Like the tigress, the lioness also was frequently
robbed of her whelps, which were reared in captivity
and destined for the amphitheatre.[3] Stories that
lions were completely tamed and trained for war
and for hunting are to be received with reserve.
Wilkinson alleges that the Egyptians " hunted with
lions, which were trained expressly for the chase . . .
and many monarchs were accompanied in battle by
a favourite lion."[4] But the picture he gives from
the tombs at Beni Hassan is far from convincing,
nor is there any written evidence for lions used
in hunting. Their use in battle is more probable,
because in that case the lion was pretty sure to die
fighting, whereas it is impossible to believe that a
lion which had struck down an antelope or other
game in hunting, and had tasted blood, would tamely
retrieve or relinquish its prey. The time must
come when the whelp, however petted, will have
its savage nature awakened, as AEschylus well knew
and tells us in the Agamemnon.[5]

Other wild animals, such as pards, wild bulls, panthers, leopards, and lynxes, were hunted or trapped
either for their fur or for riddance of a plague
and danger to the cattle on the hills. Occasion-
ally a rarer beast, such as the bison, is mentioned;

---

[1] Oppian, Cyn. III. 340-363.   [2] Id. ib. I.
[3] Id. Cyn. III. 53 mentions lion-keepers.
[4] Ancient Egyptians, I. 220   [5] Lines 717-734.

he is described as found in Thrace or Macedonia by Oppian, and the description leaves no doubt of his identity. He combines immense power with great ferocity: has a mane and a bulk which give him almost the likeness of a lion: his horns turn inwards over his head, but curve backwards with a bend like fish-hooks and have extremely sharp points, with which he tosses his foe.[1] There is evidence

LEOPARD HUNTING AND TRAP.

that bisons were regularly hunted, though towards the beginning of our era they must have become rare, and at all times they inspired the greatest terror. Some verses in the Greek Anthology[2] written by Antipater of Thrace, which must refer to a bison, show what devastation he must have wrought:

The bull which, bellowing on Orbelus' height,
    Slew men through Macedonia far and near,
Philip with lightning stroke hath killed in fight,
    Piercing its forehead with his hunting spear;

[1] Oppian, Cyn. II. 159 *seq.*   [2] Anth. P. VI. 115.

and Philip dedicated the horns and hide to Heracles. Even two centuries later Pausanias[1] tells of a bison in Paeonia which was taken by the safer method of a pitfall.   It must have become a rare animal by that time; for Aristotle speaks of its *rumoured* existence in Paeonia, under the name *bolinthus*, or locally *monapus*: and Pliny, probably following Aristotle, says that it is reported to resemble a bull, except that it has a mane like a horse's and horns that are useless for fighting—not a very accurate picture.[2]   But in an earlier chapter[3] Pliny gives the right name *bisontes* and distinguishes them from *uri* or aurochs, as does Seneca.[4]   The ordinary wild bull was common enough, and well known for his fierceness in battle with his own kind.   When two bulls meet, their bodies quivering and necks arching, they glare with eyes of fire at each other, snorting and tearing up the ground: then bellowing in angry challenge they charge headlong, and the encounter is like that of two warships in a battle at sea, when, laden with men in flashing armour, sped on by wind and oar, they crash together their brazen prows, while the shouts of men mingle with the din of rending timbers and the roar and riot of the waves.[5]   But Oppian did not regard the wild bull as game for the hunter.

Leopards, pards, and panthers are not clearly distinguished, although the panther is sometimes defined as having no spots.   Pliny seems remarkably confused about them.   In one place he says that tigers and panthers differ from other animals in having spots or stripes, while all other beasts are of a plain colour: and he compares the panther's spots to small eyes on a white ground—language which seems to show that he is thinking of the snow leopard.   Another kind of animal, the pard, very

---

[1] X. 13.   [2] N.H. VIII. 40.
[3] N.H. VIII. 15.   [4] Phaedra, l. 64.
[5] Oppian, Cyn. II. 49-64—one of his best similes.

common in Syria and Africa, is party-coloured, but as some say only distinguishable from the panther by the absence of white.[1] The same kind of confusion reigns in Oppian, who in one passage speaks of " weak and worthless beasts, like panthers and wild cats," and in another of " fierce and deadly leopards," *pardalies*.[2] But it is the leopard who figures most in legend, and while his form and markings are correctly given by that poet, much is made of the fairy tales connecting him with the origin and the orgies of Bacchus. Once upon a time they were not grim bogies of wild beasts but bright-eyed lasses, fond of wine, who carried laden vine-branches at the great festival at Nysa, and to whom the baby Bacchus was brought in a deal coffer hidden under fawn skins and clusters of grapes. He was carried into a cavern for safety, and, lest his cries should be heard by the jealous Heré, who had a most unmannerly fancy to kill him, such a hubbub was made with drums and cymbals that his loudest squalling was drowned. The goddess was completely deceived by this clever trick, never thinking that there could be anything wrong in such divine music. When all fear of danger had passed away, the nymphs took the baby in his box on a donkey down to the shores of Euripus[3]—(the strait between Boeotia and Euboea)—where they found an old fisherman with his sons, who agreed to ferry them across to the island. So the company of maidens stepped into the boat with their coffer, whereupon the benches bloomed richly with flowers of bindweed, and clusters of vine and ivy twined about the stern. So frightened were the boatmen that they were all going to jump

[1] Plin. N.H. VIII. 23-4.
[2] Cyn. II. 575 and III. 63.   See Prof. Mair's Notes on pp. 105, 118.
[3] Clearly the Nysa of this story was in Boeotia: there were at least ten places which claimed the name.

overboard, but at that moment the keel grated on the strand.

Now the king of that island, called Aristaeus, lived in a cave at the top of a mountain, but nevertheless was a very wise man in all things belonging to country life. He was the first man known to have a flock of sheep, the first to make olive oil from the wild berries, the first to make curds, and the first to take swarming bees, and keep them in hives. Lifting the child Bacchus out of the little chest, he reared him in the cave with the help of the nymphs who brought him and the fairies of the woodland. As he grew older, the boy played about with other children: but at one time he would cut a stalk of fennel, and smite the rocks with it, until from the clefts there gushed out dainty wine: another time tearing a great ram to pieces, he would scatter the little bits all over the ground, then with his magic hands he would put all the scraps together again, making a perfect ram, which went browsing about the grass.

So he went through the world, with his train of Maenads (or Bacchanal women), and revealed his gift of wine everywhere, coming last of all to Thebes: where the king Pentheus was angry and shocked, because the maidens of the place went out to greet him and to take part in the scandal of the dancing and drinking ritual. So he ordered his guards to seize Bacchus and to hale him off in chains to prison. However, the shackles fell away from the god, and the heart of the women worshippers froze with fear, so that they flung the crowns of flowers off their heads and the wands from their hands, and they wept, crying aloud: " O blessed one ! O Bacchus ! Flash forth the flaming lightnings your father wields; make the earth tremble; and bring swift vengeance upon the head of this wicked king." Their cry was heard, and the lord of Nysa turned Pentheus into a wild bull, and at the same time a change passed over the women. Their bodies became clothed with spotted hides, their eyes turned green, their jaws were armed with fearful fangs, so that they were no longer fair women but savage leopards. Pentheus had fled, but the leopards hunted him out among the rocks and tore him to pieces.

That, says Oppian,[1] *is the true story, and must be believed at heart*. There are no doubt tales told by other bards of strange doings in the glens of Mount Cithaeron and in other lands, but they are silly and wicked fables made up by idle singers.

Moreover that true history explains why leopards are so fond of wine that wine is used in the Libyan desert in hunting them. There are places there in that thirsty land where in the wild waste of sand a spring of water bubbles up in wondrous wise: it has no overflow to wander away like a stream, but where it rises it forms a small basin, and all the water that escapes from it sinks again into the sand. Such a spring is chosen by the leopards for their watering place, and they come there to drink at dawn. When the hunters have discovered this resort, they sally out at dusk carrying with them twenty large jars of fine old wine, which they empty into the basin of the fountain, making the water all purple. This done, they hide themselves as best they may under goatskins or under their hunting-nets, for there is not a rock nor a tree to shelter them, and wait for the dawn. Lured by thirst and the grateful odour of the wine, the leopards come and lap it up greedily. Its first effect is to make them dance about in a sort of drunken ecstasy: next their limbs grow unsteady and their heads giddy, so that they nod and roll over and finally sink into a deep slumber. Thereupon the hunters come out of hiding with their ropes and nets or weapons and make an easy prey.

[1] Cyn. IV. 316.

This method of taking the leopard is certainly not sportsmanlike, however curious and ingenious: but must the story be " believed at heart," like the story of the origin of the race of leopards ? A sceptic (if there is one), or a higher critic, might ask, was it not a little extravagant in the hunters to provide a vintage wine for the leopards ? for we are told that the beverage was eleven years old. Again, if the spring was bubbling up all through the night, was it not likely that the strength, as well as the bouquet and the flavour of the wine on the palate, would be somewhat impaired towards morning ? Possibly also a stray leopard or two would sometimes come too late for the feast, and, misunderstanding the pose of his fellows or the presence of the hunters, might spring upon them and cause an unseemly fracas. Still when these clouds of doubt pass away, a vein of fact with a gleam of truth will be discovered, and it must be acknowledged that leopards were taken with wine—in both senses. This particular form of hunting accordingly finds a place in the records: and nothing is more certain than that the idea of leopards as wine-lovers was widespread in the classic world and inspired classic painters and sculptors to produce some beautiful works of art.

Yet another method of capturing leopards was in favour with the Moors. They built a hut of stones, something like a den for captured animals, and within they placed a piece of rank-smelling meat fastened at the end of a long rope. The door is very lightly made of reeds and palm-leaves and allows the scent of the meat to travel abroad. The leopard revelling in it comes rushing from mountain or valley or ravine to the feast, as if drawn by a spell, charges against the door and overthrows it, and so betakes him to the fatal banquet. For a very cleverly con-trived net is so arranged that as the animal pulls at the rope to devour the meat, the net is released and falls slowly all round the walls of the hut, so that he is encompassed and captured.[1]

It is also said that a leopard hunt sometimes ended in a cage with a mirror so arranged as to attract or challenge the leopard.

But as leopards were captured by wine, so in some places where panthers abounded and threatened to overrun the country they were killed by meat poisoned with aconite.[2] Pliny also mentions that as a charm against panthers and lions the Parthian made a decoction of hen's brains and garlic—for internal application:[3] while in a third passage he tells of a people far south of Nubia called *Agriophagi* because they ate the flesh of lions and panthers.

There is proof enough that elephant hunting was practised from the earliest times both in India and in Eastern Africa—a very large trade in ivory being carried down the Nile for Europe. But there is little in the way of sporting chronicles about it, and no need to linger upon it. The same is true of the rhinoceros, which was not uncommonly seen in the spectacles at Rome.[4] The methods and machinery for the transport of such animals over long distances by land and sea, and for their feeding and tending during the journeys, prove that in such matters the Romans were little behind the modern world.

Perhaps enough has now been said about what I have called the larger game. But one comes across little pieces of information here and there, which

[1] AEl. XIII. 10. Unfortunately he does not further explain the machinery of the trap.

[2] Pliny, N.H. XXVII. 2.   [3] Ib. XXIX. 25.

[4] Martial, De Spectaculis, 22. The verses under this title give a good deal of information about the various beasts, etc., shown in the Amphitheatre. Even a stag-hunt was represented. Oppian, like many writers of his time, has a full and fairly accurate description of both elephant and rhinoceros (Cyn. II. 489-565). He speaks of ivory-turning, but is silent about the hunting or capture of these animals.

may be wrought together not without some pleasing
pattern or colour. The onager, or wild ass, was
much admired for his size, his silvery coat, his shapely
legs, and for his fleetness of foot outstripping the
wind. Oppian has a long and rather silly story of
the jealous nature of the male, which leads it to
mutilate a male foal, while the dam indulges in a long
and tragic chorus of lamentation over it, deploring
the deed of her cruel " husband." Martial speaks
of the wild ass as an object of the chase. " The
grand wild ass is here: no more hunting of the
elephant: away with all your nets":[1] which means
briefly that the chase of the wild ass is the best of
all sports. Pliny[2] gives Phrygia and Lycaonia as
good breeding grounds for them, but adds that the
young colts, which make the best eating, come from
Africa, and are called *lalisiones*: Martial has the
same idea.[3] As to the common mule, Pliny says
that frequent potations of wine prevent him kicking
—a rather ambiguous statement: but it must mean
that mules, like leopards, are given to wine: the
alternative would be that hardly a mule-driver
anywhere would keep sober.

The Nomads of Africa were celebrated above all
for their horsemanship and their hunting.[4] On their
very fast Libyan mounts they chased not only stags
and gazelles, which are run down fairly easily, but
wild asses, which have far greater pace and endurance
over vast distances. For instance during the expedi-
tion of the Greeks with Cyrus (which resulted in
the Retreat of the Ten Thousand), Xenophon records
that when they were crossing " the plains of the
Arabs," *i.e.* the Syrian or Mesopotamian desert,
they often saw herds of wild asses, but no single

---

[1] Ep. XIII. 100.   [2] N.H. VIII. 69.
[3] Ep. XIII. 97: Quam tener est onager, solaque lalisio matre
                    Pascitur.
[4] What follows is from Arrian, Cyn. 24.

horseman ever was able to capture one of them: and
when drives were arranged, in which one party of
men pushed the quarry towards another party at
some distance, even the most hardy were in the end
utterly beaten and spent. This proves that Cyrus,
son of Darius the king, had no really first-rate horses
for the chase. Yet in Libya there are boys of eight
years old or thereabouts who ride bare-back, using
merely a switch instead of a bridle,[1] and follow the
wild ass on and on and on, until at last they run him
down, fling their lasso over his neck, and he is
vanquished.

Gallant little fellows were those Moorish boys,
gallant their steeds, and splendid the training of both.
To chase the fastest animal known for long hours
over the desert, foodless and waterless, to conquer
the quarry in a desperate duel of speed and strength,
and to take him an unresisting prisoner homewards
over the same wide stretches of sand—this was an
achievement which could hardly be rivalled today
even in the same part of the world. It shows, too,
how clearly the image of war stood before the eye
of these desert hunters. When at last the wild ass
felt the noose upon his neck, he acknowledged his
defeat, in the words of the Greek writer, and followed
the victor as captive.[2] There is no doubt that these
beasts were tamed and kept in droves. Crossed
with a mare they produced an extremely fine type of
mule, and, as stated above, the flesh of the young
colt of the onager was esteemed a great delicacy.
But to recur to the image of war. Among all the

---

[1] This custom of riding without a bridle made a great impression
on classical writers. Strabo in mentioning it adds that the horses
are small, as one might have imagined: *Numidae infreni* is the
term given by Vergil (Aen. IV. 41): Livy speaks of *equi sine frenis*
(XXXV. 11): Claudian's words are *Sonipes ignarus habenae—virga
regit* (Bell. Gild. I. 439), and other instances are given by Prof.
Mair in the Loeb Oppian, p. 165.

[2] τὸ δὲ ἕπεται ἡττημένον Arrian, Cyn. l. ς.

examples which shine from classic writers on
Mr. Jorrocks' great maxims I know of none with
a clearer light than one which is given by AElian,[1]
and it concerns the same people, the Libyans.
When a man is killed by an elephant, either in
hunting or in battle, he receives a distinguished
funeral, at which dirges are often sung over him.
The burden of the chant is that the hunter has
acquitted himself bravely in stalwart fight against
a mighty foe, and that his noblest array for burial
is found in a glorious death.[2]

How reverently would Mr. Jorrocks have bared
his head, as he stood beside such a grave—yet not
without the thought perhaps that his formula for
the percentage of danger in the chase would need
some revision. But what if one can find in the
classics a word about his own favourite sport before
quitting this subject ? In the opening chapter
I remarked that fox-hunting was unknown as a
pastime in the ancient world: and it remains true
that the mystery of fox-hunting, with all its apparatus
of art and science and its code of laws — to say
nothing of riders galloping across green valleys or
rising over stone walls or fences—had no counterpart in classic times. Yet it is curious that Oppian
in the very last lines of his poem on hunting speaks
of *the wily one*, as the fox was often called in Greek,
in these terms: He is not to be caught by lying in
wait, nor by snaring or netting, being much too

---

[1] V.H. XII. 52.

[2] τὸ ἐνδόξως ἀποθανεῖν ἐντάφιον εἶναι τῷ θαπτομένῳ. Among
Greeks and Romans alike it was customary to clothe the body of
the dead in his best robe, and very costly fabrics were used for
a funeral of honour given to men of high station or renown. But
a further illustration from AElian is worth quoting. Xenophon,
he says, had a great regard for beautiful weapons. He used to say
that for a victorious general the most brilliant equipment was
appropriate, and that a soldier fallen in battle rested most nobly in
full panoply: that was the burial array (ἐντάφια), which truly
reflected his glory (V.H. III. 24).

clever not to notice such devices, and he has his own artful tricks of gnawing through a rope or untying a knot, and slipping away in sly escape from death. But when a whole pack of hounds is after him, they toss him at the last, though, staunch as they may be, for them it is no bloodless victory.[1] Sometimes perhaps a hunt was organised beforehand in places where foxes were doing a great deal of damage: sometimes, as in Thrace, foxes were hunted for the pelt, of which caps were made: and sometimes hounds were drawn off, when following other game, by the scent or view of a fox. But it cannot be doubted that the men in such a chase knew something of the sport, something of the joyous excitement, of the fox-hunter today. And unquestionably the same thought flashes out in the poet's line about autumn—not as the " season of mists and mellow fruitfulness "—but as the " season of hounds and hares and foxes."[2] So Martial, though he speaks rather of fox-hunting in Italy and the damage which the fox will do to hounds, yet proves that the chase there was of set purpose and no mere accident. The run was made to end in a net, where reynard was brought to bay and killed, but it was followed with whoop and halloo and music of hounds.[3]

[1] Cyn. 448-453.

[2] καὶ κυνῶν αὐτῇ τόθ' ὥρη καὶ λαγῶν κἀλωπέκων, quoted by Athenaeus, VII. 282, from Ananius (540 B.C.).

[3] Martial, Ep. X. 37:

> Hic olidam clamosus ages in retia vulpem,
> Mordebitque canes sordida praeda tuos;

and Nemesianus, Cyn. 52, nec vulpem captare dolosam Gaudemus, *i.e.* our delight is not in fox-hunting.

CHAPTER VII

FISHING

Early Records—Sea-fishing—Royal Sport—Oppian's Treatise on Fishing—Homer—Mr. Radcliffe's Work—Sacred Fish—Plato on Angling—Aristotle.

IT may give a little disappointment to the angler of today to learn that in the classic world fishing meant principally sea-fishing. But truth must sometimes be told—even by an angler writer to an angler reader. And if tapered casts, check-reels, split-cane rods, and dry-fly fishing were mysteries unrevealed to the Greek or Roman, he had an amazing knowledge not only of other mysteries of his own craft but of marine zoology in general. This latter was founded mainly on Aristotle, who, according to the well-known story of Pliny, had an army of researchers working for him by land and by sea—an army which was subsidised by Alexander the Great, and which achieved such conquests in the realm of nature as outshine and outlast all his victories on the field of battle. Sea-fishing, then, must take the foremost place in this essay, but later on there will be something to say about fresh-water fishing, and also about fly-fishing.

The question may be asked, was there any real feeling of delight, any sense of sport, in sea-fishing ? Mr. Radcliffe, whose great work on Fishing from the Earliest Times[1] is known to every angler and every scholar throughout the world, would answer

[1] London, John Murray, 1921 and 1926, p. 72 (2nd edition). The writer somewhat modifies his opinion in one or two other places.

No: " Hunting, fishing, and laying snares for birds in Homer and even in the classical periods had but one aim, food."[1] I have shown, conclusively I hope, that the idea of sport was not only present but predominant in hunting. The case is not so clear for fishing, and much at first sight tells against it.

SEA CREATURES.
From a mosaic.

Artemis is seen by Homer delighting in her bow and quiver, as she ranged the hills in joyous chase of boar or deer in company with her sporting maidens.[2] She is called queen of the sea by Euripides, though at the moment he would seem to have been thinking rather of the seashore: but there is at Athens a very

[1] Ib.   [2] Od. VI. 102-106.

archaic vase from Boeotia,[1] on which a figure alleged
to be Artemis is painted with a fish on her dress,
wild beasts beside her, and fowls above, as if she
were patroness of fishing and fowling as well as
hunting.   But I think the fact that even as early as
Pindar she is called ποταμία is not without significance
(Pyth. II. 7).   Poseidon, Pan, and Hermes were also
regarded as presiding over the fisherman's fortunes.
Yet there is no sense of radiant joy in their sove-
reignty, as in Homer's picture of the huntress queen.
Poseidon was merely king of the ocean, and galloped
over the waves drawn by sea-horses or dolphins:
Pan comes in as warden of the wild—whether on land
or water: and Hermes finds a place as bringer of good
luck—a thing which all anglers stand in need of.
But none of these deities thought about fishing as
a pastime.   Oppian himself, too, contrasts fishing
unfavourably with hunting.   The hunter, he says,
meets a bear or a boar face to face, and watches his
chance to shoot or to spear him at close quarters:
he has hounds moreover to track and mark down
the quarry and to help him in the encounter.   He
fears neither the heat of the sun nor winter's rage,
for he finds shelter in shady thickets or cliffs or
caves, and has never-failing springs to quench his
thirst: in short, there is far more pleasure than hard
work in hunting.[2]   But the toiling fisherman has no
sign to guide him or to mark his prize, no hounds to
discover the quarry, no shelter from rain or storm,
from burning heat or icy cold.   He is driven at the
mercy of wind and wave, and scared by monsters of the
deep.   His only strength is in hair-lines and hooks
and rods and nets, and " unstable as a dream is the
hope that flatters his heart "[3]—surely an eternal truth.

[1] Mr. Radcliffe gives a cut of this vase: see pp. 126-7, and his
notes.
[2] Hal. I. 28.
[3] Prof. Mair's admirable rendering of this line is quoted: the
rest is a paraphrase, not preserving Oppian's order.

Nevertheless there is royal sport and keen delight
for the Emperor when, seated in his light but well-
braced galley, he is sped by powerful oarsmen to an
open reach where the waves are gently rippling.
The water teems with fish which have been well fed
and fattened, and the Emperor lets down a fine-spun
line with bronze hook baited. No delay: the bait
is seized: and a fish is pulled up quivering and
wriggling—which is great fun for the Lord of Earth
to behold. . . . The poet here is thinking of one
of those salt-water preserves—perhaps a small cove
or inlet shut off from the sea—such as rich nobles
under the empire were fond of enclosing. But as
for sport in this royal pastime—as well sit in a punt
on the Thames and fish for gudgeon.

Rightly enough the term θήρα, or hunting, is often
used in description of fishing, and the element of
search for the quarry, the use of surmise and imagination, the finding, and the capture, are all essential
to the idea of sport—of which poor Marcus Aurelius
can have known nothing. The element of danger,
while not by any means essential and in some forms
of sport almost unknown, does none the less add
a zest to the day's work, and, if for this reason alone,
I would say that the toilers of the sea know the
meaning of sport. But even where there is no
danger, sport is not sport, or at least has not the true
savour of sport, without an element of adventure.

It is with this thought as guide that I propose
to deal with Oppian's great Treatise on Fishing.
His catalogue of fishes and other marine animals,
with notes on their haunts and habits, is an astonish-
ing piece of work, however much he may owe to
previous writers, and one must believe him when he
remarks that the sea had been explored in his time
to a depth of three hundred fathoms. But many of
his fish cannot now be identified, although Prof.
Mair's able research has done much to " illumine

the depths of the sea ": and in any case this is not
an essay on zoology, but deals rather with the
weapons and methods of fishing in vogue, and perhaps
with some picturesque or dramatic episodes in the
fisher's life.

One cannot escape, however, from going back to
make a start with Homer, about whose fishing-lore
some strange and beautifully pedantic things have
been written.   First, it has been said, that neither in
the Iliad nor in the Odyssey is fish put on the table
at banquets: therefore Homer makes his heroes
abstainers from fish: and therefore fish was not
known as food in Homer's time or in the time in
which he sets his scenes !   What a feat of logic is
here.   Yet, as Mr. Radcliffe points out, Homer
represents his ideal king as reigning in righteousness
over a mighty people, where the soil is rich with
corn, the trees are laden with fruit, where cattle
thrive, and where the sea yields store of fish.[1]   Cattle
and corn and fruit and fish—all presumably for the
table.   Yet apparently there is no mention even of
fruit in the diet of heroes in Homer: and Athenaeus[2]
tells us that fish and fowl and fruit are omitted lest
there might be a loss of dignity in such detail, or lest
a charge of gluttony might lie against the heroes !
Considering that the heroes were not ashamed to
feast the livelong day, nor was Homer shy of recording the fact, the explanation of Athenaeus is rather
witless.   The truth is that all these phantoms of
doubt can be laid by a word of common sense:
Homer was not writing a bill of fare.

To the argument that fish was not eaten in Homer's
age or was not fashionable, an answer equally decisive
may be given.   One has only to recall the fact that
in the primæval legend of Greece fish is spoken of
as a delicacy: for it was by promise of a feast of fish
that Zeus lured Typhon out of the monstrous pit

[1] Od. XIX 109-113.   [2] Deip. I. 16, 22, and 46.

in which he dwelt in the bowels of the earth, and so
was enabled to crush his hundred heads with thunder-
bolts.[1] The one thing in which such a myth cannot
lie is that fish was considered a dainty for the gods.
The like inference may be drawn from a passage in
Athenaeus, who alleges that the people of Elis wor-
shipped Apollo as the Fish-Eater:[2] and on an Attic
vase of about 500 B.C. Poseidon, Heracles, and
Hermes are drawn all fishing together.[3] There is,
then, no period in Homer in which fish was rejected
as food or despised by the wealthy. Nor is there any
force at all in the argument that fishing or sailing was
not among the scenes on the Shield of Achilles.
A crazy logic may ask, Why are they not shown
there ? The simple answer is, Why should they
be shown ? The space was small for the whole of
life.

However, it is just worth remarking that Hesiod's
Shield of Heracles does represent a fishing scene
—a harbour with rippling waves, a school of dolphins chasing fish, and on the shore a fisherman
watching and waiting, in act to cast his net.[4]

Even the critics, however, do not challenge the
fact that in Homer rod, line, net, and fishing-spear
are quite familiar weapons. It is true that they are
usually found in similes:[5] but this only means that,
while the poet was not writing upon the art of angling, he chose his comparisons from such practice
of the art as would be within common knowledge
and would come home at once to his hearers or
readers. There is, however, one mystery in the
Homeric fisherman's craft, one item in his outfit,
which may have been well understood by the poet's
contemporaries, but which has never since his time
been understood at all. Both in the Iliad and in

[1] This story is from Oppian, Hal. III. 18-26.   [2] VIII. 36.
[3] Fishing from the Earliest Times, p. 11.   [4] Lines 207-215.
[5] Fishing from the Earliest Times, p. 74.

the Odyssey the horn of an ox is mentioned as mounted with lead and attached to the fishing-line.[1] The fisherman perched on a jutting rock flings the horn into the sea, where it falls with a loud splash and sinks to the bottom. In the Iliad the horn carries death down to ravening fish, the swift descent of the lead sinker being the chief point in the simile; while in the Odyssey it carries luring baits for small fish, and the angler is using a long rod. Mr. Radcliffe[2] has tried this puzzle from every side with every aid available for dexterous handling, and there is no need to follow here his careful analysis of the several solutions which have been offered. One thing, however, seems to me quite certain—that when Homer spoke of the horn of a field ox, he meant an oxhorn, and did not mean a little tube of horn to protect the line above the hook, and did not mean a fish-hook made of horn, or any other trifling toy in the angler's equipment. My own solution, for what it is worth, is as follows. A long rod, which Homer postulates, would require a longer line, and, there being no running rings on the rod, the line could not be thrown out as far as might be necessary by action of the rod. On the other hand a horn, when weighted for sinking, would be very easy to handle and to fling to the distance desired. In other words the horn was used *for convenience of casting*. A short length of line, armed with one or more hooks hung below the horn, and the fish to be captured were either those that haunted the rocks or flat-fish lying on the bottom. Homer represents the fisherman as jerking or swinging (ἔρριψε) his prey out of the water— a fact which might suggest possibly that the hook was not barbed: but such an inference would be quite unwarranted. The barbed hook is very ancient, and just the same bad style of landing a fish

---

[1] κέρας βοὸς ἀγραύλοιο, Il. XXIV. 78-82; Od. XII. 251-254.
[2] Pp. 81-84.

is recorded by Ausonius on the Moselle twelve centuries later.[1]

There is no real inconsistency between the ravening fish of the Iliad and the small fish of the Odyssey passage. *Ravening* is not a measure of size: it is used in a quite general sense in Oppian— " savage beasts and ravening fishes "[2]—and means little more than voracious. But the meaning of the epithet ἱερὸς applied to a fish in another passage of the Iliad has been, and is, vainly disputed. Of the explanations offered, not one is really satisfactory. One is that very frequently in Homer and later writers the word ἱερὸς means nothing but strong or fine, with little or no religious connotation. An instance of this sense may be found in the Hippolytus of Euripides, where the mighty tidal wave which struck the shore and brought the hero to death is called ἱρὸν κῦμα;[3] but there perhaps the idea of divine agency may just possibly be present and the sense would be given by *portentous*, if the image of that word were not too worn away in English. On the other hand, Homer cannot have thought of any really big fish, for no such fish could have been landed with rod or line by a lonely fisherman, nor are such monsters often found close to a rocky shore.

It is urged, however, that the term ἱερὸς ἰχθύς, which I venture to render *hallow fish*, has a specific or technical meaning, and denotes a particular kind of fish. In the main that is true, but unfortunately the name is given to several kinds or tribes. Aristotle says that the *anthias* is called a hallow fish and that its presence is taken by sponge-divers as proof that the water is uninfested by sharks or the like: but in another passage he remarks that some people call the *aulopias* a hallow fish: Oppian gives the

---

[1] Ad Mosellam, l. 255-8.
[2] Hal. I. 704-5. Prof. Mair renders *carrion* fishes: but the sense surely is eating raw food, not rotten food.
[3] Hippol. 1296,

name to the *callichthys* or fairfish: and elsewhere
the dolphin and the pilot-fish are so distinguished.
Now it so happens that all these are big fish and deep-
sea fish, and not one of them could possibly have been
landed by an angler seated on a rock with rod or line,
still less flung out of the water. To Homer, therefore, the ἱερὸς ἰχθὺς did not denote any particular
species of fish: it probably meant nothing more than
a *goodly* fish. But the meaning of the term holy
fish or hallow fish and the meaning of the oxhorn
in Homer lie sunken in the depths far beyond all
hope of recovery through any instrument of modern
criticism.[1] It is as well to acknowledge the fact and
pass on.

It must be acknowledged also that if the idea
of sport ever crossed the mind of the Homeric angler,
it finds no expression in the Homeric poems—a fact
which might lead a modern angler to exclaim,
" What a measure of the blackness of the darkness
of that dark age !" But, once again, the silence of
the poet cannot be taken as a proof of ignorance: it
does not follow that because Homer never paints
a merry angler either by river or by sea such a being
was unknown in his day. It has even been urged
by some writers that the phrase *merry angler* is a
contradiction in terms, so far as the classics are
concerned. It is true that the conventional fisherman of poetry is generally a poor old creature who
dwells in a rude hut of reeds by the shore, and barely
contrives to make a living by ceaseless melancholy
toil at imminent daily peril. But though sometimes
true in its own limited setting, such a picture, if
taken to represent the angling world of the time, is
a mere child's caricature.

----

[1] It is just possible that the epithet ἱερὸς in Homer and later
writers was derived from Syrian beliefs. The Syrians did regard
fish as sacred, and Xenophon (Anab. I. 4. 9) in passing with his
Ten Thousand through North Syria came to a river in which tame
fish abounded and were not molested by the natives.

Set beside this grotesque drawing and gloomy colouring another picture furnished by no less an authority than Plato—a picture which is shown only for a moment and then withdrawn, but which still lives as an imperishable proof of his belief in the joys of angling. In his Book of Laws, in a passage I have already cited, he is considering the value of various forms of sport for the education of young men, for the improvement of their mind, body, and character, and in short for the development of qualities required in the ideal citizen. He comes to the conclusion that hunting—incessant hard work in the field with constant bracing in the peril of personal combat—is the only form of sport which can be encouraged by law: but what does he say about fishing? He represents himself as speaking to a class of young Athenian pupils of his own rank, *in terms of earnest entreaty*,[1] as follows: " I pray that no yearning, no passionate love, of sea-fishing, or of angling may ever take possession of you, my young friends." Plato's objection to these forms of sport was that, compared with hunting, they were rather idle recreations which required no feats of endurance, and gave no training for bodily prowess, or self-control, or calm and courage under stress of danger. But he does *not* say that angling is a contemptible amusement or a trade fit only for ancient and impoverished mariners. On the contrary, the very fact of his imploring his young hearers not to be carried away by a passion for fishing is a decisive proof that he considered such a passion natural and normal, and that many young men of the day were keen anglers.[2] And as I have said that Plato's audience were young fellows of good family and good

[1] δι᾽ εὐχῆς. I have rendered the passage at more length on p. 26 above, and given the reference to Plato, Legg. VII. *sub fin.*

[2] The words ἐπιθυμία and ἔρως are both significant of the powerful attraction which angling did or might exercise: no stronger words could be found.

intelligence, who had no thought and no need to go fishing for a livelihood, it follows that their motive was pure love of sport, and that angling as a form of sport was fully recognised. It is not surprising that we hear so little about it, or at least about fresh-water angling: for there were no fishable rivers in Attica, the Cephisus and Ilissus being mere brooks, with no continuous stream of water flowing down to the sea, and elsewhere in Greece the rivers were seldom at any time of the year constant enough in level to furnish good fishing-grounds, nor did their plunging torrents and rocky channels encourage breeding and growth of fish or the practice of riverside angling.

Here, then, is discovered one definite reference in Plato, writing about 400 B.C., to the amateur angler, and the discovery is made by accident, as has happened more than once previously during research into the methods and apparatus of hunting. For there is no treatise on fishing in Plato's time, and it is a long way back from Plato to Homer. Nevertheless, granting that this one instance is authentic—which seems undeniable—and granting that the conclusion I have drawn from it is as sound in fact as in logic, it needs only a moment's thought to carry the figure of the amateur angler back to a date far earlier than Plato. For Plato does not speak of the sport as a new attraction for young men or a new invention of his age: he merely takes it for granted as one of the ordinary temptations of the day, which were likely to waste the time and dissipate the energy of those whom he wished to see trained by harder forms of sport to fitness for the service of their country. And the methods of angling and the tackle in use in Plato's day were almost certainly traditional from a much earlier antiquity.

Nor can one trace any break in the tradition for some centuries after Plato. Aristotle, who wrote about fifty years later, has left a great mass of information upon living things in the seas and the rivers. His work on Natural History is the greatest work of original scientific research in the ancient world—but he has told us nothing fresh about the art of angling: from which it is fair to argue that there was little or nothing fresh to tell. Nor is there any evidence of new discovery or improvement in the art from Aristotle's day down to Oppian's, while much of the lore and much of the practice in vogue when Oppian wrote remains unaltered to this hour, as the modern Greek writer, Apostolides,[1] has shown.

[1] La Pêche en Grèce, Athens, 1907. Prof. Mair quotes freely from this work.

CHAPTER VIII

FISHING : ARTS AND ENGINES

Qualities Required—Ingenious Devices—Plato Again—Seasons
for Sea-fishing—The Rod and its Nature—Cane and Greenheart—Hand-lining—Lucian's Angling Stories—Hook and
Line—Weeling—Fishing by Torch-light—Poison.

IN opening the third book of his poem on
Fishing Oppian bids the Emperor to note the
ever-changing wiles of the fisher's art, the fisher's
feats in combat with his prey, and the set ordinances
of the deep. He then calls upon Hermes as chief
patron of the brotherhood : for Hermes was the first
to open the gate of knowledge for the fisherman
and to teach him the manifold aim and purpose of
the craft. In the previous book[1] he had made Hermes
patron of eloquence and athletic sport, and given
the sway of the ocean to Poseidon, with a possible
reserve for Nereus or Phorcys : but it did not matter
so long as some divinity was present to manifest
his power—and different gods have different parts
to play in the world. Yet he adds that as fishermen
seek first the favour of Hermes, so by Hermes' help
he will sing the story of their deeds.

To be successful, a fisherman must be active and
strong of body, with sound clean limbs, having
endurance necessary for long spells at sea and sinews
fit to grapple with big fish when they are writhing and
plunging. He must have wit, too, to counter the
tricks to which fish resort when surprised by strange
contrivances : must be dauntless, cool, and resource-
ful : a light sleeper, keen-sighted, with mind alert

---

[1] Hal. II. 27-37.

and eyes open. He must be hardened against winter's cold and summer's heat: above all he must be fond of work, and love the sea.[1]

Such is Oppian's man, and how unlike the dreary and decrepit figure of convention. He must have been a fine fellow, the type of seaman familiar to us all round the shores of England, storm-proof and battle-proof. It is by no accident that the poet makes love of the sea his crowning quality: for just as love of hunting is essential to the sportsman on land, so delight in sea-faring must run all through the fisherman's life on the deep. It may be said, that is all very true, but what room is there here for any idea of sport? Is it not merely professional fishing that the Greek writer is concerned with? and how does his fisherman differ from one on a Brixham trawler today? Two answers may be given. First, the answer founded on Plato's evidence that sea-fishing did in fact appeal to the young Athenian as a form of sport, and, although he discouraged it, his teaching could never have suppressed it or robbed it of its charm for future generations: next, it must be remembered that in classic times sea-angling was carried on with a variety of method and diversity of ingenious devices which surpass anything employed in modern times—at least in northern waters—whence arose in amplest measure incidents, excitements, and surprises, which gave a decidedly sporting character even to the professional calling, and which formed the charm for young men of good birth in search of pleasure and adventure.

And here two quotations may be given from the Letters on Fishing by Alciphron, who was about contemporary with Oppian. In one of them[2] the writer says: " I never knew how pampered and luxurious are the sons of rich Athenians till the

---

[1] Wakefulness and love of work are combined in Soph. Ajax, 879-880. [2] Ep. I. 15.

other day, when Pamphilus and his friend hired our
little boat, the sea being calm, to join us in sailing
and fishing." They lolled about under an awning on
rugs and carpets—in fact formed a water party with
girls and music, caring for nothing but amusement.
This doubtless was the kind of thing against which
Plato warned his pupils. In the other passage[1] a
sailor writing to his wife says: " To us who have
our life on the sea the land is death, just as it is to
fish out of water "—proof enough that love of the
sea was real: and one may add that a third letter is
addressed to Θαλασσέρως, or Lover of the Sea.

There seems good reason to suppose that when
Plato appears to distinguish angling from sea-fishing,
the distinction to him was real. The word rendered
by *angling* is ἀγκιστρεία, which is generally taken
to mean fishing with a hook, ἄγκιστρον; but as Mr.
Radcliffe has shown, the Greek word denotes originally rather a bend or an angle than a hook, and
though it acquired later the more limited and specific
meaning of a bent metal hook, it still might nevertheless have stood in Plato's thought for something
like *Fysshynge with an Angle*. This belief is strengthened by the passage in The Sophist[2] in which
Plato sets himself to analyse the term ἀγκιστρεία,
and defines it as fishing with a rod and line in such
a way that *striking* becomes essential, *i.e.* striking
with a barbed hook and pulling a fish out of the
water. It is true that this process is as easy and
familiar on sea as on land: on the other hand, in
the Book of Laws Plato definitely sets all forms
of sport by sea in antithesis to angling, using the
most comprehensive term possible, ἡ περὶ θάλατταν
θήρα, for the one and ἀγκιστρεία for the other.
If this be so, there is sound reason for thinking
that with Plato *angling* generally meant not only
rod-fishing but *fishing in fresh water*. The same

[1] Ep. I. 4.   [2] Soph. 220 d.

SEA-PERCH, ETC.
From a Pompeian mosaic.

To face page 132

distinction seems to be drawn by AElian,[1] who, speaking of various forms of catching fish, says that *angling*, ἀγκιστρεία, is not only the most skilful form but the one most becoming to gentlefolk, and it can be shown (as I hope to do later) that he is thinking of fresh-water fishing. This conclusion may not stand so clear that no shadow of doubt can pass over it: but it is upheld by the actual wording of the law which Plato lays down for the regulation of fishing generally, whether by land or by sea. To cover both kinds, he coins a special word, ἐνυγροθηρευτής, for which there is no equivalent in English: *hunter-by-water* is nearest, *water-sportsman* rings a little truer, but neither is flawless. However, the canon of the law is that this fisherman-in-general " is forbidden to fish in harbours or in *sacred*[2] rivers, marshlands, or lakes, but may lawfully fish in all other rivers and lakes, provided that he shall not cloud the water with drugs." These last words may prohibit the practice of using poison and apparently apply to fresh water; for " clouding "[3] could hardly apply to the sea, although poisoning fish in the sea was not very unusual. Thus of a particular poison called πλόμος, *i.e.* mullein or verbascum, Aristotle remarks that its use for taking fish in rivers and lakes is general, but that the Phoenicians use it for sea-fishing.[4] On the other hand Plutarch, who wrote some four centuries after Aristotle, while using the same word for cloud-

N.H. XII. 43.

Pausanias, I. 3. 21, mentions a lake at AEgine in Laconia, which was sacred to Poseidon and was never fished.

[3] It is curious that Plato does not speak directly of poison. His word ἀναθόλωσις means *discolouring* by some decoction, ὀπῶν, and it may mean merely clouding very clear water to make the angler and his tackle less conspicuous. But would an innocent practice have been forbidden ? Of course it may be that ὀπῶν is from ὀπή and not from ὄπος, and the expression would mean discolouring the fishes' *holes* : but that is very improbable.

[4] H.A. VIII. 20. 3.

ing as Plato, explains the process: a man carrying
a bladder filled with a dark liquid lets out some of
it into the sea, when he wishes to escape notice: a
casual remark, which implies that by that time the
use for sea-fishing had become quite an ordinary
practice.[1]

Two points, however, may now be considered as
proven: first, that in the earlier classical writers
fishing was by no means understood as sea-fishing
exclusively, and next, that angling was regarded, or
was capable of being regarded, as a form of sport.
Doubtless as a sport it was not so widely recognised
as hunting, because it did not require the same bodily
training or resourcefulness or activity, nor did it
offer the same excitement, as hunting: moreover it
was not readily available, like hunting, at almost all
times and places for its votaries.

After all, it must be remembered that so far the
scene has been set mainly in the fourth century B.C.
or earlier, and it would be unreasonable to expect
that either the art of angling or the sense of sport
had developed very fully at that period. But that
both did develop in the course of the next five
hundred years will be shown hereafter. Here for the
moment let one of the younger Pliny's letters be
cited,[2] which he opens by asking his friend Caninius,
" Are you reading? or fishing? or hunting? or all
three together? For all three are possible at my
house—fish in the lake, game in the woods, and
the deep seclusion of the place for study." It is
the letter of one country gentleman to another,
typical of the life dear to both, in which reading
and outdoor sport were happily blending: but that
the fishing here was for pastime and sport alone is
beyond all question. So the Emperor Augustus
used to go fishing, as Suetonius relates, *animi*

---

[1] De Soll. An. XXVI.
[2] Ep. II. 8.

laxandi causa, as a diversion from the cares of
State.[1]   And Venus did not fish for " the pot."

But it is time to return to Oppian and sea-fishing.
He recommends morning and evening as the best
time in autumn, sunrise in winter, while in the
spring fishing is good all day long.   Some fishermen
use rod and line, the line made either of twisted
horsehair or of finely woven flax, the latter probably

VENUS FISHING: CUPID EXCITED.
From a Pompeian painting.

as fine and as strong as any ordinary line in use
today.   The rod is constantly described as long,
length being necessary to keep the line well clear
of rocks or of the boat: it had a natural bend and
taper, being in fact a stout cane from a lake-side
plant which, though called a reed,[2] was tall and
strong enough to resemble bamboo.   But the nature

[1] Suet. Aug. 83. 96.
[2] λιμνοφυὴς δόναξ in Anth. P. VI. 23: κάλαμος also is common.

of the rod has been rather a mystery. No other plant than bamboo would obviously fulfil the required conditions of length and strength and pliability: and all but waterside plants are excluded. Yet the bamboo was not indigenous to Greece: and if it was ever imported, it cannot have been imported as early as Homer, who speaks of a *very long rod*. Mr. Radcliffe alleges that the reed was imported from Abaris in Lower Egypt, and he makes AElian say that *juncus marinus* and *ferula* were used for heavy fish.[1]

It is fairly obvious, however, that the nature of the fishing-rod or rods used in classic times offers a problem which, as far as I know, has never been solved. For example, if AElian said that *juncus marinus* made a rod capable of dealing with heavy fish, he was plainly wrong: for it does not produce any growth strong enough for the purpose. Pliny[2] gives a full account of that plant (called ὀξύσχοινος in Greek) and its varieties, the strongest being that which is named ὁλόσχοινος, but this is described by him as "soft (or pliable) and fleshy:" the cane is used for making fish-baskets and vine-trellis, and cane as well as pith for lantern lights. There is not the least suggestion that the stalks in any form could be used as fishing-rods. Yet in another passage Pliny says that the choicest reed for fishing-rods was the reed from Abaris in Africa.[3] AElian in his description of tackles required for various forms of fishing remarks,[4] first, that the plant is useful for making weels, and next, a few lines

---

[1] Page 236. I have not found the passage in AElian, nor the authority for this statement.

[2] N.H. XXI. 69.

[3] Ib. XXI. 66: Aucupatoria arundo a Panormo laudatissimaː piscatoria Abaritana ex Africa. One cannot say whether Panormus in Sicily was intended or not: and if Abaris was the rather obscure place in the Delta of Egypt, why does not Pliny write *Egypt* instead of the vague *Africa* ?

[4] N.H. XII. 43.

lower, speaking of its reeds as dry and soaked, clearly distinguishes them from the two rods which the angler wields, and of these rods he calls one a rod of *narthex* (which is to be trimmed or polished), and the other a rod of cornel wood. Now this is somewhat interesting. The *narthex* corresponds, as Pliny tells us, to the Latin *ferula*, and *ferula* is a particular kind of reed from which a light cane rod might easily have been made, though not one which would serve for heavy fish.

But there is another plant of the reed family, which is of much stronger growth. It is known today as *arundo donax*, a botanical name which curiously combines the most familiar Latin with the most familiar Greek term for rod. This is a native of the Mediterranean region and is by far the largest of European reeds. It has a cane which is knotted,[1] grows sometimes to a height of twenty or thirty feet, and has a thickness to correspond. Though it has been called the bamboo of Europe, it is not a bamboo but a reed, botanically. Here then we have an explanation of the " very long rod " of Homer in the discovery of a cane which gives the lightness and the length required.

I think, then, it may be taken as settled that both *ferula* and *arundo donax* furnished canes which were made into fishing-rods by Greeks and Romans, but that the *ferula* produced a rod considerably shorter than the other.

But the interest of AElian's passage does not end here. He speaks definitely of a rod of *cornel wood*, and I know of no earlier mention of such a rod.[2]

---

[1] Pliny, N.H. XIII. 42.

[2] Greek κρανεία, called τανυφλοιὸς in Il. XVI. 767, *i.e.* long and slender. The word served for javelins, Homer, H. Merc. 460, and spear-shafts: ξυστοῖς κρανείοις πρὸς πάλτα ἐμάχοντο: they fought with cornel spears against hurled javelins, in Arrian Anab. I. 15. 5: also arrows were made of cornel. Vergil has *Itala cornus* (AEn. IX. 698), and *stridula cornus* (ib. XII. 267).

Here again Pliny helps to an understanding. After
speaking of ebony, box, and other hard woods, he
mentions cornel as too slender in growth for use as
timber, but as having so close a grain that there was
no better wood for making wheel-spokes or wedges
or bolts, being almost as hard as iron. Putting
together the evidence of these two writers, one is led
irresistibly to the conclusion that cornel wood, with
its characteristic qualities of slenderness and tough-
ness, furnished the material for building a new kind
of rod, which should be stronger and more powerful
than any weapon of reed.   It furnished in fact a
greenheart rod, which was an entirely new development in the angler's tackle, and though it did not
supersede his *donax*, or cane rod, it greatly widened
the sphere of his art and increased its pleasure.

If there were any doubt about this distinction
between the *calamus*, or cane rod, and the cornel,
or greenheart, it must yield to the evidence of
another passage in AElian. He is giving his own
version of a man fishing for sargues in the guise of
a goat, and he makes the matter a little clearer than
does Oppian.[1] The fisherman ground-baits the
shallow pool with a paste made of barley meal and
goat's flesh; then, standing so that the sun throws
his goatish shadow on the water, he waits while the
sargues assemble. His line is white or grey and
carries a stout hook, and *his rod is not a cane but a
cornel rod*, because when he has hooked a fish he must
pull him out at once without resistance, since to play
him would frighten the others away. In other
words the cornel was the stiffer and more powerful
rod.

The use for *rod* is unknown to Pauly's Real-Encyclopädie,
and to Liddell and Scott, and the word is not to be found in Daremberg.

[1] N.H. I. 23. Oppian, for example, merely speaks of a *rough
rod*, but its purpose is the same—a rapid haul to avoid alarming
the shoal.

Yet another kind of rod was used by the Carians in fishing for the same sargues. When a soft wind blows from the south, when the waves are becalmed, and a light ripple plashes on the sand, then the fisherman has not the smallest use for his cane, but takes a *rod of juniper of the strongest possible description*[1] and fishes with pickled anchovy for bait. Here the object is the same, to land the fish at once on striking.

Clearly the calamus, or cane rod, was a *whippy* rod and quite useless for certain kinds of fishing. For, as Plutarch says,[2] Fishing is no simple or trifling matter, but requires for its practice all sorts of instruments and accomplished knowledge of clever and ingenious tactics. Thus the rod (*calamus*) must be slender, though it must be springy (ἔντονος) enough to bear the strain of a plunging fish, but a light rod is essential, as a heavy one would cast a broad shadow and alarm the fish. The line, too, must not have many knots or be coarse, as this would betray the cunning design: moreover the hair cast next above the hook must be as near white as possible so as to resemble the colour of the water.

In the Geoponica of Dionysius an angler is spoken of who fishes with a pair of rods, each carrying a line with four hooks: he has an attendant or gillie with him, and is warranted by using proper bait to land more fish than any netting could provide.

The problem of the rod, then, if not finally solved, is brought as near to solution as possible: and it needs no stretch of imagination to picture the Greek or Roman angler of the second century starting out

---

[1] AElian, N.H. XIII. 2. The words are ἀρκεύθου ῥάβδον πάνυ σφόδρα ἐρρωμένης. Cornel presumably was not obtainable, and a stem of juniper served for the rod, if one of great strength were at hand. AElian in the words I have given above is in a half-poetic mood, but he has a great command of Greek and a strong imagination. The juniper was probably the *Oxycedrus*.

[2] De Soll. An. XXIV.

for a day's fishing armed with a well-built and well-balanced greenheart. Later I hope to show that the rod was jointed.[1]

Hand-lining from a boat was a common practice, and the hand-line was sometimes furnished with a number of hooks—perhaps like the poacher's *otter*—trailing near the surface, and sometimes sunk with a plummet of lead to catch deeper-running fish. Nets were of all sizes and shapes—casting-nets, drag-nets, trawls, seines, ground-nets, ball-nets, and, as Oppian says, there are a thousand forms of nets with cunning entanglements. Weels were a favoured device with some fishers, weels which gladden their " owners while they slumber in peace and bring much profit with little toil."[2]

But rod-fishing was very often practised from a river bank or from a rock jutting out into the sea. In the preface to his poem on Hunting Oppian describes the typical angler as sitting calmly on a rock by the shore with bending rod and deadly hooks, and his delight when he strikes a fish and sweeps it high into the air—another instance of that bad style of snatching which has been noticed before, and which apparently has the sanction of Homer. Such a style would be impossible with any but small fish : there is, however, proof in The Fisherman's Dream of Theocritus[3] that the skilful playing of a heavy fish was familiar enough. Here the fisherman—the very type of the poor and miserable toiler of the sea common in fiction—is sitting on a rock, with eager eyes scanning the water, as he lowers his bait. It is seized by a fish " of the lordly sort ": he strikes: the rod bends almost to breaking with the strain: and a far-ranging battle begins. When

[1] In the chapter on fowling: pp. 185-190 below.

[2] This is precisely why Plato denounces weels, using the same word, κύρτοι, and saying that they catch fish for which the owner does nothing.

[3] Idyll. XXI.

A FISHING COMPETITION.
From a Pompeian painting.

To face page 141.

the fish sulks, a touch of the hook sets him off, and the line is slackened correspondingly: as the run ceases, the line is tightened: till in the end the angler wins, and lands " a golden fish, a fish one solid mass of gold." The hook is gently removed lest any of the gold should come off with it, and the fisherman says, " Here is the fish I have dreamed of all my life: never again will I kick my heels on the sea: I shall play the king with my gold on land."

It is a pretty story and true to nature in the main. Most anglers today can tell the story of their golden fish; some can tell the tale of many: but so far from the gold becoming tarnished with time, it gleams and glows brighter and the fish grows in weight, as the story is told and retold.

Lucian too is fond of fishing stories or allegories: two of them, one from his Fisherman and one from Hired Company, are worth quoting. In the former[1] a group of the chief philosophers have dismissed their audience on the Acropolis, a miscellaneous rabble whose devotion to virtue and wisdom is questioned by high personages such as Candour, Truth, Philosophy, and an Examiner. A test is proposed, with a wreath of olive for the true believer, and a branding-iron to stamp *fox* or *dog* on the brow of the charlatan. They have gone; but Candour offers to bring them back, and borrows from a temple (in which they had been dedicated) rod and tackle, and from the priestess also dried figs and a piece of gold for bait, to catch gluttony and avarice. Candour takes his seat on the Acropolis wall and makes a cast over the city below: whereupon Philosophy asks if he is trying to fish up blocks of stone from an ancient building there. " Hold your tongue," is the reply, " and wait till you see the catch. Here comes a big basse, or a gilt-head perhaps."

[1] ἁλιεύς.

" No," says Examiner, " a cat-fish. He is going open-mouthed for the hook. He smells the gold: now he is on to it, seizes it, is hooked. Up with him."

" Well, lend a hand with the line: up he comes. And pray, my excellent fish, what are you ? This is a dog-fish, a cynic: Heavens, what teeth !¹ So, my noble friend, you were caught hunting dainties among the rocks where you thought you could not be detected. Plain enough now, hung up by the gills: but look, the hook is bare, and he has bolted the fig and the gold."

" Make him disgorge," says Diogenes.

" Very good," is the reply, " but do you know this gentleman ? is he one of your following ? No ? Well, I put him down as worth about twopence: and you ?"

" Too much: he is uneatable, hideous, tough, and worthless. Fling him head foremost down the rocks, and try another cast; but mind that your rod does not break with the strain."

" No fear, Diogenes, they are a light race, lighter than sprats. But look ! what is that flat-fish ? He comes up like a fish cut in two—a sort of plaice—gapes, and swallows the hook. Hoist him up."

" What is he ?"

" He calls himself a Platonist."

" Scoundrel," cries Plato, " and you in search of a piece of gold ? Hurl him down the cliff."

Bidden by Diogenes to try again, Candour says: " Now there comes a real beauty (as far as I can judge in such deep water), rainbow-hued, with gold stripes on his back.² This fellow pretends to be an

¹ The κύων, sea-dog or dog-fish, is always described as one of the monsters of the deep, and was probably one of the lesser sharks. Needless to say that the term *Cynic* is derived from κύων.

² An allusion to Aristotle's alleged fondness for rings, jewels, and plate.

Aristotelian. He comes along, then shies off, looks carefully all round, comes on again, seizes the bait, and is swung in the air."

Aristotle denying all knowledge of him, he is flung down the rocks again, and Candour remarks: " Now I see a shoal of fish, all the same colour, prickly and horny-coated, harder to catch than sea-urchins. We want a net for them and there is none at hand. Enough perhaps if we catch one of them, and it is sure to be the bravest that takes the bait."

" Make your cast, then," says Examiner, " but you must first arm your line some way above the hook with wire, or he will swallow it and then bite the line in two."

So the fishing goes on, one pretender after another taking the bait, until at the end the philosophers decide that there is very little to be done with the crown of olive and very much work withal for the branding-iron.

The other scene, from Hired Company,[1] represents a man being cautioned against capture by parasites who angle for him. " Whenever you hear language like this, they have seen you opening your mouth wide for the bait. It would be wrong for us to let you think that, although we saw you about to swallow the big hook with the prawn upon it, we would not lend a hand, nor jerk it away before it stuck in your gullet, nor even give you warning: but would stand there, watching as the hook is struck and fastened in your jaw, so that you were dragged and pulled along, utterly powerless, and none the better for our idle tears." So they proceed to tell their friend about all the devices of the anglers—nets, weels, quite unescapable curved hooks with barb returned, prongs of the trident spear, and such like: he should puff out his cheeks, and try if the hook is not very sharp, very unbreakable, very unpleasant

[1] περὶ τῶν ἐπὶ μισθῷ συνόντων.

in fact, as it tugs violently at the wound and holds irresistibly.

There are in these stories two points worth special notice. First the mention of arming the line to prevent its being bitten through. The Greek word σιδηροῦν implies the use of iron, which must mean either a small tube of iron to cover the line or iron wire woven about it: but the latter meaning seems far more likely, as from the context the protection has to reach some way up the line, ἐπὶ πολύ, and

CUPIDS FISHING.
From a Pompeian painting.

with a tube such an arrangement would result in clumsy or unworkable tackle. This danger of the line being bitten through by a shark or other big fish was very present to the mind of fishermen and was met by various devices. One such device against the *amia* is mentioned by Oppian in a passage which has been strangely misunderstood.[1] To avoid this danger

ἐχαλκύσανθ᾽ ἁλιῆες
καυλὸν ἐπ᾽ ἀγκίστρῳ δολιχώτερον,

[1] Hal. III. 147-8.

which Prof. Mair renders " forge a longer *socket*
on the hook," while Liddell and Scott give *fishing-
rod* as the meaning of καυλόν: but what meaning
they could have given to the whole sentence the
wisest head in the College of Anglers will never
discover. The sense is very simple: καυλὸς means
the shank of the hook, and this is lengthened, so
that the teeth of the fish will meet on the shank and
not on the line. The other point is the casual
mention of the prawn, not merely as used for bait,
but as an ordinary bait with anglers, although
Oppian, rather oddly, makes out that the prawn is
used for small fish.[1]

A word may be said with regard to the double
bait dangled on the line which Candour throws
from the wall of the Acropolis. It is curious
perhaps that dried figs should be regarded as a
luscious morsel to tempt a glutton and should be
used to typify luxury, as the gold typifies love
of money. The fig may be merely a suggestion
from συκοφάντης—a word of which the derivation
has never been satisfactorily explained: yet seven
centuries before Lucian gold and figs are set in
contrast by the poet Ananius in the lines—

> εἴ τις καθείρξαι χρυσὸν ἐν δόμοις πολλόν,
> καὶ σῦκα βαιὰ καὶ δυ᾽ ἢ τρεῖς ἀνθρώπους,
> γνοίη χ᾽ ὅσῳ τὰ σῦκα τοῦ χρυσοῦ κρέσσω.

But the point of interest to anglers rather is the
arrangement of the two baits. The context tells
against any opinion—in itself unlikely —that the
fig and the gold were both on the same hook:
either then a double hook must be imagined, *i.e.*
two hooks with a single shank, or two indepen-
dent hooks, one set higher on the line than the
other, like a dropper. On the whole, judgement

---

[1] Hal. III. 177. Possibly here a shrimp rather than prawn is
intended.

must go in favour of the double hook, *i.e.* not a
hook with two barbs, although that form is found,
but a shank with two hooks arranged in the form of
an anchor.[1] So much for rod and line, though there
will be more to say when we come to trout fishing.

As to the weel, Plato's contempt for this kind of
sport, or rather idleness, was based on the fact that
it was merely *trapping*, and gave no scope for the
exercise of manly qualities. AElian, perhaps con-
sciously, takes the same view, for he speaks of
weeling as a game of low cunning, a sort of shameless
conspiracy against good fish, and a pursuit hardly
fit for gentlemen. This condemnation has more
force as bestowed on river-fishing than on sea-fishing:
for the term would include lobster-pots as well as
the long hooped weels used for various sea fish.
Oppian describes a way of catching the *admon* which
sounds ingenious. A weel of osiers was lowered
with a pierced stone to serve as anchor, but was held
off the bottom by corks, which floated on the surface.
Four small stones covered with some sort of sea-
slime were placed inside the weel, and a number of
small fish were soon collected there to feed on the
slime. The admons, eager in turn to feed on the
little fish, rush into the weel, only to see their prey
slip away between the osier ribs, while they remain
imprisoned. Something of the same device is used
against the *salpae* which feed on seaweed. The
fisher chooses his spot, and for four days running
ground-baits the place with seaweed fastened to
stones: on the fifth day he takes his weel, disguised
with green growths and carrying inside the favourite
weed wrapped in stones, lowers it and leaves it
for a while, allowing time for the fish to enter. The

---

[1] See Mr. Radcliffe, p. 238. The wording in Oppian, Hal. III.
285-7, is obscure, but does not, I think, imply a double hook. Only
a single hook is mentioned and the γλωχίνες, which hold the rope
on each side can hardly be *barbs*, as Prof. Mair renders, but are
clamps with teeth which grip the line and hold it fast.

oars are muffled and no word is spoken: for the
salpae are easily scared, and " silence is an advantage
in every sort of fishing.''[1]

Large weels were also used to catch the sea-bream.
These weels were made of broom or withys and had
a very wide girth: were baited with broiled crayfish
or the like—the savoury smell being thought to
attract the victims—and set slanting among rocks.
It was another waiting game, but when the trap was
full, the door was clapped down, and the weel
hoisted up.

There is, however, a way of boat-fishing with a
weel, which has not quite the same taint of idleness,
and has a touch more of sport. Two men row the
boat, while of two others, who form the crew, one
tows along a female parrot-wrasse on a line—alive
if possible. If the fish is dead, then a leaden weight
called a dolphin is fixed in its mouth and on another
part of the line a heavy sinker of lead, so as to imitate
the movement of a live fish in the water. The other
man tows a large weel, through which apparently
the line with the decoy passes: and when the male
wrasses throng after the female, the decoy is pulled
into the weel, the wrasses rush in after her, and there
is no returning from that house of death.[2] Weels
also were placed on the beach in the spring and
covered over with green foliage for the capture of
cuttle-fish, which were attracted to them as likely
shelters in the breeding season. They were also
used in winter by the side of rivers in a rather
curious manner. In the dry season a trench was
dug with one end opening on the riverbank and was
roofed over with dead grass and stones. Weels
were set inside it, and in winter fish, avoiding the
deep water of the now swollen stream, moved
up the trench for shelter and were captured.[3]

[1] Hal. III. 429.
[2] Hal. IV. 75-110. The phrase of course is Oppian's.
[3] Aristotle, N.H. VIII. 20. 4.

Spearing fish with a three-pronged spear or trident was a common occupation, practised alike on land and on water, by day and by night. In day-fishing from a boat, the weapon used was sometimes short in the shaft but attached to a long cord: it was hurled with great force and amazing dexterity so as to strike fish deep in the water below. AElian has some curious remarks on this form of fishing, which he calls κόντωσις,[1] *i.e.* poling. The word should mean punting; but although punting may come in just before the trident is launched, the fishermen are described as requiring a long boat, manned by stout rowers who keep good time together, and hempen cords are also mentioned. But as pine-torches are also part of the outfit, AElian must have been thinking of night-fishing with the trident. In any case he calls this the most manly form of sport, as requiring great strength and endurance, as well as skill, in the angler. But this night-fishing with blazing torches was often carried on without anything in the nature of harpooning. Torch or cresset was set on the bows of the boat, which was allowed to drift or was gently propelled until fish were lured near enough, when a long-handled trident without any cord attachment was used for striking. It is worth noting, however, that instead of blazing pinewood sometimes a brass lantern[2] with sides of horn was carried on the prow of the boat, but presumably only on calm water. Plato alludes to this as *fire-fishing* in the well-known passage in The Sophist:[3] Scott describes the same sort of sport in Guy Mannering[4]: it runs through the literature of the ancient and the modern world, and is found in almost all countries as well as all ages. The flare, however, was and is still

[1] N.H. XII. 43.
[2] Oppian, Hal. V. 430: ἵπνου χαλκείοιο θοὸν σέλας.
[3] 220 d.
[4] C. XXVI. It was sometimes called *leistering*. Redgauntlet gives an account of hunting and spearing salmon on horseback.

used to decoy fish, as well as to spear them. The
boat is turned round and round several times, then
as the bewildered fish crowd towards the light, it is
very gently moved up to a shelving beach, as close
as possible without touching, and nets are swiftly
flung out to encircle the prey.

Countless other wiles were devised against the
denizens of sea and river. Two may here be added
to the list, both of a most unsportsmanlike character.
For the capture of flat-fish a short thick log or roller
of wood was prepared, covered all over with three-
pronged spikes, and weighted at both ends with lead.
A rope was fastened round it, as it was launched
from a boat and plunged into deep water, where it
pierced and held any living thing it encountered.
As it was quickly raised to the surface, fish were seen
tossing and writhing in torture: and it would, says
Oppian, rouse compassion in the hardest heart to
witness the unsportsmanlike manner of their capture
and death.[1] This cruel and repulsive form of fishing,
as he calls it, was in vogue with Thracians to the west
of the Chersonese, and his language here shows a
sense of fair play, a humanity, and a resentment
of wrongful methods, which mark him as a true
sportsman.

Scarcely less emphatic is his condemnation of
poisoning as a way of taking fish—a way still known
in the Mediterranean. He seems, however, to think
it rather a pretty device when used with a weel to
entrap certain fish like the shark. A cake made of
vetch-seeds, parched and seasoned with rich wine
and myrrh, is put inside the weel, which is dropped
and anchored in the sea. Quickly the scent as of
lilies runs through the water bringing a message to
varied shoals of fish, who throng towards the sweet
savour till the weel is filled.[2] There is certainly
nothing cruel or revolting in this procedure: but

[1] Hal. IV. 521-550.　　　　[2] Hal. III. 398-413.

the use of wine is curious.   Mr. Radcliffe[1] gives an
illustration taken from a mosaic at Melos, in which
a fisherman sitting in his boat is holding out a long
pole with a vessel of wine at the end: around him
various fish, including mackerel, conger, gurnard and
lobster, are thronging and tumbling: but there is
nothing to show how he catches them, unless per-
chance it be by a casting-net which he carries across
his shoulder.   Wine, nevertheless, is not always
a very bad poison, even in these days, and one may
assume that the fish, even if they drank of it like
fishes, entered into their captivity with nothing
worse than a premature sense of exhilaration.[2]

Very different was the way of the real fish-
poisoners.   They gathered a small fleet of boats
outside some rocky cove which they encircled: then
by flinging stones and beating the water with poles
and oars they drove all the fish within the cove,
to take shelter among the crannies of the rocks.
The mouth of the creek was then completely blocked
by a ring of netting, and a fisherman leapt over the
enclosure, carrying in his hands two cakes made of
powdered chalk kneaded into a stiff paste and
poisoned with cyclamen, with which he wandered
round, smearing all the cells and chambers in the
rock, till the foul bane of his loathsome ointment
defiled all the sea.   Having done the work with his
deadly drug he returns to his boat.   Very soon the
hateful odour reaches the fish in their recesses:
their eyes are dimmed, head and limbs turn giddy,
and they rush in terror out to open water, where
like drunken things, reeling under the deadly fumes,
they plunge about hither and thither, seeking in vain
escape from their grievous plight, and hurling them-

[1] Page 241.
[2] In the *Geoponica* of Cassius Dionysius, who translated the
Carthaginian author Mazo (88 B.C.), Book XX contains a large
number of prescriptions for compounding baits, very many of
which are mixed with wine.

selves against the nets in hope to break through. But there is no deliverance from doom, and no relief. Darting and leaping they roll about in pain, and as they perish a sound of sighing passes over the waves —the only lament for their fate. Merrily the boat-men wait, heedless and heartless, till the noise of plashing and battling is over, the last sad breath is breathed, and silence falls upon the sea. Then the fishers gather up countless heaps of dead, all slain together by one befouling doom.

Such is Oppian's language. It is true to fact, as one who has seen fish drugged with a less fatal in-toxicant can testify: and its tone of tragic drama is preserved in my rendering. Nothing is more cer-tain than that the poet was moved by the deepest pity and indignation against the fish-poisoners: and if one jot of doubt remained, it would be removed by the comparison which follows, when he likens them to men conducting a siege who poison all the water-springs, so that the whole city is cumbered with the dead, who have perished by a rueful and dishonourable doom.[1]

He makes clear the distinction between sport and slaughter even in sea-fishing.

---

[1] Hal. IV. 647-693. In Pliny XXV. 54, the use of an even more deadly poison is mentioned. The tuberous root of the aristolochia—which was called ground-poison—was pounded and made into a paste with chalk or lime, and he had seen this scattered on the sea by Campanian fishermen. Fish rushed at it greedily, but were killed immediately and floated dead on the top of the water. Pliny also mentions one of the cyclamens *qua pisces necantur* (XXV. 69).

CHAPTER IX

SOME LARGE FISH

Anthias—Swordfish—Tunny — Whale-fishing—Dolphin — Silurus
of the Danube—Fishing with a Team of Cattle.

THE nomenclature of the fishes in classic
writers has been studied in modern times and
various tables of identification have been drawn up,
with the result that a good deal of room for guess-
work remains. This is true no less of the larger
than of the smaller fishes: but the difficulty need not
deter one from recording some few stories of hunting
the big game of the sea.

The *anthias* has already been named by Aristotle
as, in the opinion of some, the same fish as *aulopias*,
but there is little clue to its identity. Aristotle calls
it a gregarious fish: and its presence denotes water
safe for divers. Oppian describes it as haunting the
rocks and caves on the coast of Cilicia, his native
province. Ovid tells of its turning head downwards
when hooked and sawing through the fisher's line
with sharp tooth-like projections or fins on its back:
and it was said also that one anthias seeing another
caught would rush to the rescue and cut the line
in the same manner. AElian makes out the aulopias
to be a monster fish, and says that although not so
large as the largest tunny, yet in strength and fighting power it has the advantage: it meets the fisherman in a fair duel and very often defeats him. In
Cilicia there were two ways of catching the anthias.
A fisherman having discovered a place under the
cliffs haunted by the fish, rowed up to the spot and
made a din by clapping two boards together, where-

upon an anthias came up and looked about curiously.
The fisherman at once threw out sea-perch or crow-
fish as food, which was readily taken. Day after
day the fisherman repeats his visit, until the fish
learn to expect the good things he offers, go to meet
his boat gaily, and gather about it unafraid. They
become so tame that they feed out of his hand and
move in any direction to which he points. In due
time he gets ready a strong line and hook, marks
one particular fish, and waves the others away with
his hand or sends them diving after stones. He
lowers the baited hook and captures his victim
which he hauls into the boat triumphant. But it
requires a powerful man or two men to pull him in,
as it must be done quickly before the other fishes
can detect the scurvy trick that has been played
upon their comrade. This method of fishing would
seem to show that the anthias of the rocky shore
was a fish of good size, doubtless, but not a
monster.

There was no such crafty stratagem in the other
method of hunting the anthias. As soon as one was
seen on the surface, a fisherman in the stern of the
boat paid out his line—a stout rope, having a double
hook, baited with a basse. He kept the bait gently
moving until it was seized by a good fish. Then
began a fierce battle, the fish plunging and pulling:
the man holding the line, bracing and straining
every muscle in his brawny frame to prevent him
diving. The crew now falling on their oars and
rowing their hardest, he leans backward to get a better
purchase, the line sings as it cuts the water, and it
tears through his hands till they are covered with
blood: but he holds gamely on, like a wrestler who
never loosens his grip. The shoal of anthias, now
aware of their comrade's plight, rush to the rescue,
tumble all over him and try in vain to break or saw
through the line. Their mouth is unarmed, but

sometimes the hooked fish contrives to saw and rasp
through the cord with his jagged spine, and sails
away. Otherwise the fisherman keeps a tight line,
never yielding an inch, till he tires the anthias to
death and pulls him into the boat.[1] Other big
fish like the fairfish or beauty-fish and sharks are
taken by the same method.

The waters of the southern coast of Gaul, particularly in the region of Massilia, or Marseille, abounded
in swordfish, which elaborate measures were taken
to capture. Boats were built in shape like the quarry,
with long narrow hulls and at the bows a toothed
sword under or on the water. The swordfish are
deceived by the likeness and come up fearlessly,
when the fleet of boats encircles them and a battle
begins. Many of the fish are slain easily by the
trident which strikes at close quarters: others fight
bravely, and a boat is often rammed and the hull
pierced clean through by a sword. The crew at
once ply pole-axes to hew off the sword, but it
remains fixed like a rivet in the timbers of the
vessel while the fish is grappled with and hauled
aboard. Sometimes, however, the swordfish is
surrounded by nets and gradually forced ashore,
never having the sense to charge and tear through
the meshes with the weapon it carries.[2] Strabo
gives a rather different account of hunting the swordfish as practised off the eastern coast of Sicily. A
number of small boats, each manned by two fishermen, await a signal from a watcher on the cliffs, and
put out to meet the swordfish. The man at the
bows carries a sort of spear with the shaft loose in
the socket. When he plunges it into a fish, the shaft
of the spear is withdrawn, while the barbed spear-
head remains embedded in the flesh, but is made

---

[1] Oppian, Hal. III. 205-334. Like the anthias, the beauty-
fish cannot be identified.
[2] Id. Hal. III. 542-575.

fast to a long cord which the fishermen hold, and they play the fish to exhaustion.[1]

One of the largest, the most prolific, and the most voracious of Mediterranean fishes was the tunny; it came in at regular seasons from the Atlantic. Vast shoals worked their way along the northern shores, by Gaul, by Italy, Sicily and Greece to spawning-grounds in the Euxine, and spread all over the sea. The time of their arrival in spring is well known, and in likely places along the coast which they have to pass, watchers are perched on lofty look-outs, whence the number and size of the shoals is signalled to the fishermen below, who hasten out and set ring upon ring of nets, in which great multitudes of fish are taken, and " rich and rare is the spoil."[2]

The value set upon these huge coarse fish is rather remarkable. The tunny at the present time has its lines of travel far up the western coast of Norway on one side and on the west of Ireland on the other, as well as in Indian and American waters. It is very destructive of salmon and other good fish: it often breaks up nets in which it becomes entangled: but it is sometimes hunted today as a food-fish, having as such a market value. But in classic times there was an enormous trade in fish of the choicer sorts, both dried and pickled in brine, all over the Mediterranean, as well as in fish sauces and dainty conserves of many kinds. It may be that tunny and swordfish came in for their share of this trade: for in a big catch they could hardly be used as fresh food.

The whale, however, must have been hunted for the same purposes for which it is hunted today. The wonder is that such a serious business was undertaken with so frail an equipment: but, apart

---

[1] Strabo, I. 16. He also gives an alternative name γαλεώτης for swordfish, but the identity is clear.

[2] Oppian, Hal. III. 620-648. Prof. Mair gives very interesting notes from AElian and the modern Apostolides.

from its profit, it appealed to hardy and sport-loving seamen as a trial of skill and a dangerous adventure. The recital of the hunt in Oppian[1] makes rather a long story, but one which is worth telling—with some abridgement.

All the monsters of the sea, except the dogfish, are cumbered by their bulk and weight, and roll about the billows slowly in their travels. Nature, however, has provided them with a guide and friend, the leader or pilot-fish, as it is called, which has a long, dark body and a long slender tail. The pilot—all eyes and ears—guards the whale, signals the way to food, warns him of shallow water, and alarms him at any threat of danger. Accordingly, the whale-hunter's first task must be to capture the pilot-fish, which is done with a baited hook. It is to be presumed that a particular whale must have been marked beforehand and his movements studied: otherwise how could the pilot-fish be discovered and captured ? At any rate the monster now roams about, defenceless, helpless, and so blinded that he often is stranded on the shore. Then begins the chase, and keen are the fishers' thoughts, as they make ready their tackle. Strangely enough, the capture is not made by harpooning, but with a baited hook. A finely-woven but strong cable, as thick as the forestay of a ship, ends in a length of chain, which is fastened to the butt of a large hook. The description of the hook is not very clear; but it is enormous, strong enough to tow a rock or to pierce through a reef, and has two or more curved limbs armed with double barbs. The chain, wrought of hammered bronze, is long enough to prevent the formidable teeth[2] of the whale from cutting through the cable, and it is ingeniously set

---

[1] Hal. V. 62 *seq.*

[2] The sperm-whale is said to be the only Mediterranean whale furnished with teeth, and so must be identified here.

with a number of swivels, which keep both chain and cable from twisting, however the sudden and violent coils and contortions of the fish may strain them, as he rolls and tosses or plunges. On board the boats are stored a number of tridents, pole-axes, and harpoons, *i.e.* iron javelins with a ring at the top through which a line of rope passes.

With muffled oars they advance stealthily, until they are near enough to fling out the hook, which is baited with the liver or shoulder of a bull. The jaws of the monster open to swallow the bait: he feels the barbs driven into his throat, and in pain shakes his head, vainly striving to break the chain. Then he dives deep, and the cable is paid out with the utmost speed; for the fishermen know that he could drag them, ship and all, to the bottom. Lashed to the line are several large balloons or air-filled skins,[1] which run out and sink with it, but hardly retard the downward rush of the whale: but as he lies in the depths and weakens, he feels their upward pull and rushes upon them, only to see them rise out of reach as he nears them. Furiously he rages, tossing up blood and foam, while the noise of his heaving breath sounds like a storm-wind under the sea. All round the water roars and gurgles and swirls with yawning eddies, which part the billows, like the whirling surges of Charybdis. Thus for a long time the fruitless struggle continues: but, before the finish, one of the fishermen takes the shipward end of the cable in a small boat, which he rows ashore and moors it firmly to a rock—a risky proceeding, one would imagine. He returns to his ship: and now when the dread monster is worn out with the fight and drunken with pain, as his fierce spirit is yielding, and the scale of death is turning against him, then the first of the balloons floats up,

[1] In fish of less magnitude dried gourds were similarly tied to the line as floaters.

telling of victory to the fishermen and cheering their
hearts. One after another the skins rise out of the
water, and all the boats row up with noise of onset
and shouts of encouragement. Tridents and hal-
berts, spears and axes, are carried by all hands,
as the battle line advances on the whale, who has
no strength left to crumple up the boats, but with
the mighty sweep of his fins and the sway of his tail
he hollows out the sea, driving great billows against
the boats like a storm-wind and hurling them back
stern-foremost, so that all the labour of the oar and
all the valour of the men is undone. Undaunted,
they cry aloud, and renew the fight, plying their
weapons till the whole sea boils and foams with the
monster's blood, his strength is gone, and his life
is failing. Then they take him in tow, and hale
him onward, studded all over with spears, to the
land, where his last floundering avails not, and he is
stranded on the beach.

Then follows in Oppian a description of the
people ashore standing aloof in awe, slowly overcoming their fear, and drawing close to gaze in
wonder at the ruin of that mighty form, his yawning
jaws with ranges of huge teeth, his vast bulk from
head to tail, the gaping wounds, and the thicket of
spears planted upon him. A landsman among the
crowd cries out, " Dear mother Earth, who hast
bred me and fed me upon the land, in thy bosom
let me die, when my day of doom is before my face."
He wants no peril of storm, no death by wind or
wave, and above all no ending in the maw of a
giant fish.[1]

We in turn may wonder at the daring and skill
of the fishermen who with very slender equipment

---

[1] This story of the whale-hunt is somewhat condensed from
Oppian's long account in Hal. V. 92-349. Similes and some other
matters are omitted, but the rendering otherwise is as much translation as paraphrase, and it did not seem right wholly to abandon
in prose the poetic tone of the original.

could accomplish such a triumph. Though the term *ships* is used once or twice in the original story, there is nothing whatever to show that the craft used in the chase were other than rowing-boats: it is always the oar, and never a sail, which brings the fishing vessels to the encounter and works them in all their manœuvres. Some of the boats, no doubt, were heavy ones: for they had to find room for large coils of cable with the balloons attached, and for a crew to pay out the cable, or to ease its furious running as the whale dived. Weapons too had to be carried and some store of food. Other boats, however, were very light and seem to have been manned by two sailors only, as in less dangerous forms of fishing. One would think that here the risk of death was enormous, and the bold fellows who faced it with joyous excitement deserve all admiration.

It is curious to reflect that the writer of the Book of Job must have seen something very similar. The parallels in Ch. XLI. (upon the leviathan) are very remarkable. The long line of rope with a hook, the forest of javelins on the back of the monster, the fish-spears, or tridents, on his head, and the terrible teeth, are all found in this passage. Was whale-fishing known in the Mediterranean at that epoch ?

Dolphins were regarded with a sort of reverence, as well as affection, not merely in the folklore, but in the daily life of the ancient world. Their shapely forms, their ease and grace of movement in the seas, their playful gambols round the bows of a sailing ship, and their friendliness to man, gave rise to many legends, such as that of Arion, and many stories vouched as authentic, such as the friendship of a dolphin with a boy on an island near Lesbos, which Oppian says crowds stood on the beach to witness. No wonder, then, that he himself declares the hunting of dolphins to be wicked, and the slayer of a dolphin is abhorred of heaven, cut off from all service of the gods, and is a defilement even to his own household.

Yet, for all his gentle ways and his love of man, the dolphin is hunted by reckless and ungodly dwellers in Byzantium and in Thrace—men of iron heart, who would show no mercy to their own fathers or brothers or children. They put out in a light boat, and find a pair of young dolphins sporting with their mother. The young ones are unafraid, never thinking that kindly men would have hearts of guile, or devise any ill against them, and they play about the boat. Thereupon one of the villains in the crew hurls a three-pronged harpoon and the stricken dolphin plunges deep into the sea. The fishermen follow, paying out the line, and waiting till exhaustion brings the victim up to the surface. The mother dolphin remains, drives away her unwounded offspring for safety, scorning safety herself, and moving in company with her captive child, unflinching to the end, she shares its death.

This story is told by Oppian at much greater length and in very moving terms. Tender pity for the dolphin and fierce indignation against the god-forsaken scoundrels who kill it are blent together with tragic force. It may not be quite clear whether he regards these men chiefly as sinners against the laws of heaven, or sinners against the laws of humanity, or sinners against the laws of sport: but the three crimes are laid to their charge, and in the poet's opinion they are dyed with a stain which all the waters of the world will never wash away.

But monster fish were not confined to the sea; they abounded also in some of the rivers. The largest of all was the silurus or glanis—now called *Silurus glanis*, or sheat-fish—which sometimes attained a weight of 300 lbs. and a length of ten feet. It was

best known in the Danube, though found also in the
Strymon of Thessaly, in the Maeander and other
waters of Asia Minor. If Ausonius is to be believed,
it was also a denizen of the Moselle.[1] Obviously
such a fish was not easy to deal with in the channel
of a river; but AElian[2] records a very curious way of
capturing him which was in vogue on the Danube.
There a riverside fisherman sets out with a pair of
oxen (or of farm horses) carrying the yoke himself,
and wanders along the bank until he comes to a place
which looks like good fishing-ground. Then he
fastens a strong rope to the middle of the yoke, puts
the yoke on the shoulders of his team, and gives them
a good feed. The rope or line is a long one, and on
the other end he rigs up a very large and terribly
sharp hook which he baits with bull's liver, while
some way above the hook a leaden weight is attached
to the line to steady it[3] and to lessen the direct strain
on the yoke. The bait is duly flung out and, sinking
to the bottom, is seized in no great time by a silurus,
who rolls over in delight, unwitting that he has
swallowed the hook. Discovering his error he jerks
and shakes the line violently. Thereupon the fisherman, overjoyed by the signal, leaps up from his seat
on the bank, renounces all his riverside business and
all sport of angling; like an actor changing his part
on the stage,[4] he starts his team of cattle, and a fierce
tug-of-war begins between the monster fish and the
farm animals. The silurus of the Danube is a very
heavy and powerful fish and puts out every ounce of
his strength, while the oxen pull hard against him,
putting a tremendous strain on the line. But the

[1] Mos. X. 136 *seq.*   [2] N.H. XIV. 25.
[3] That is the meaning of ἕρμα, which is often used in the sense
of ballast. Mr. Radcliffe's version gives " to serve as support
for the pull," and he suggests ἔρυμα. But the lead weight makes
it more difficult for the fish to plunge about or to pull directly on
the yoke.
[4] From fisherman he turns into farm-hand ploughing a stubborn
furrow.

fish has the worst of it and is beaten in the pulling-
match: then in the end, his strength being spent,
he is hauled up on the shore. A reader of Homer
might say that it was like a waggon-load of oak
timber being drawn by oxen and mules for the
funeral pyre of Hector.[1]

The literary touch given by AElian in this allusion
to Homer is not a bad ending for a good angling
yarn. Undoubtedly fishing for the silurus with
a team of cattle was a most original idea, and playing
the fish must have been fraught with excitement,
which culminated when the fish was landed: then,
however, the cattle-driver must have forgotten his
farm work, turned angler again, and rejoiced in his
mighty sport.

In Bloch's Histoire des Poissons,[2] there is a fine
coloured print of *silurus glanis*, which gives an
excellent idea of the size and fighting power of this
giant fish.

[1] Il. XXIV. 782-4. The whole passage from AElian here has
been closely rendered.
[2] Berlin, 1795, facing p. 194.

CAR AND DOLPHINS.
From a Pompeian painting.

To face page 162.

CHAPTER X

FLY-FISHING

AElian's Description—The River *Astraeus*—New Translation of
the Passage—Trout—Singing Fish—Nature of the Horsetail
Fly—Other Notices of Fly-fishing—Materials—Goat Skin—
The Ticino Grayling—Martial—Flies for Sea-fishing —
Salmon.

IF the Thracians were always known for their
barbarity, and if in Oppian's eyes one of their
worst crimes was dolphin murder, most foul and
most unnatural, to the west and on the other side
of the peninsula of Chalcidicé were people of a
different race and a higher civilisation. Macedonia
has been mentioned more than once as famed,
among other things, for various forms of hunting:
but perhaps its greatest claim to honour in the
world of sport is founded on the fact that from
Macedonia comes the first specific or detailed record
in angling history of fishing for trout with the artificial fly. The record was written by AElian, is now
well known, and has been fully and fairly set out in
Mr. Radcliffe's great work: but the story cannot be
omitted here, nor would it be right to give a mere
copy of his version, which is one adopted from
Mr. O. Lambert's rendering "with some altera-
tions." Though on the general bearing of the
passage there is little room for disagreement, my
own translation has a good many, and not unimportant, points of difference. It is as follows:[1]

"There is a form of fishing in Macedonia of
which I have heard and have knowledge. Between

[1] AElian, N.H. XV. 1.

Beroea[1] and Thessalonica runs a river called the Astraeus containing fish of a speckled colouring: as to their local name you had better ask the Macedonians. They feed on flies which hover about the river—peculiar flies, quite unlike those found elsewhere—not resembling wasps in aspect, nor can one match them rightly in shape with what are called *anthedons* or wild bees, nor with hive bees: but they have something in common with all these. They rival in boldness an ordinary fly: in size you might rank them with wild bees: their colour is modelled from the wasp, and they buzz like bees. The people of the place invariably call them *horsetails*.

" These flies settle on the stream in search of their special food, but cannot avoid being seen by the fish swimming below. When, therefore, a fish detects a fly floating on the surface, he swims towards it very quietly under water, taking care not to stir the water above, which would scare his prey. So coming close up on the side away from the sun, the fish opens its mouth, snaps the fly down its gullet, like a wolf seizing a lamb from the fold, or an eagle seizing a goose from the farmyard: and then retreats under the ripple.

"Anglers are aware of the whole procedure, but never by any chance use the natural fly as bait: for when the flies are handled, they lose their proper colour, their wings are battered, and the fish refuse to feed upon them. Anglers accordingly leave the flies alone, resenting their cursed behaviour when captured: but they get the better of the fish by a clever and wily contrivance of their art. They wrap dark red wool round a hook and tie on to it two feathers which grow under the wattles of a cock and resemble wax in colour. The fishing rod is six feet

---

[1] Beroea was an important town on the lower slopes of Mount Bernius, and on a tributary of the Haliacmon river. It was about 30 miles from Thessalonica.

in length and the line the same. When the tricky
fly is lowered, a fish is attracted by the colour and
rises madly at the pretty thing that will give him a
rare treat, but on opening his jaws is pierced by the
hook and finds poor enjoyment of the feast when he
is captured."

Such is AElian's story of fly-fishing—not new to
the angling world, yet still possessing claims to
exceptional interest and justifying some remarks.

First, the river Astraeus seems unknown to geo-
graphers. St. Paul must have crossed it on his way
to Beroea, and one may imagine him resting beside
it. But it was clearly a small river, with broken water
and pools alternating, as is proved by the remark
about the trout retiring under the ripple. Why does
AElian not give the local name for the trout, when
he knows so well the local name for the fly ? It is
curious, but the truth seems to be that there is no
recognised name in Greek for trout. Pausanias[1]
speaks of trout in the rivers Aroanius and Ladon,
both rivers of Arcadia, the latter famed for its clear
water and regarded as the most beautiful river in
the Peloponnese. They were called ποικιλίαι, or
speckled fish, a word like AElian's κατάστικτοι.
Pausanias records a curious legend that the trout in
the Aroanius sang like a thrush. All the local people
believed it; but, he adds: " I saw them taken by
anglers, yet I never heard one sing, though I waited
till sunset, which was said to be their chief singing
time." It is strange to think that the same belief,
which Athenaeus records of the Ladon and Cleitor,
also Arcadian rivers, survives today, as Sir J. G.
Frazer relates, not only among the peasants but even
among educated Greeks of the locality, one of whom
spoke of hearing a "low musical note" from the trout.
Aristotle believed that fish had hearing and smell,
but no voice, though they could in some cases make

[1] VIII. 21. 2.

a sound. He treats fully of these noises, and says
that as birds make a noise with their wings in flying,
but that is not a voice, so not one of these noises
made by fish denotes a voice.[1] And in another place
he says of fishes, οἱ λεγόμενοι φωνεῖν, οἷον ἐν τῷ
Ἀχελώῳ, ψοφοῦσι τοῖς βραγχίοις ἤ τινι ἑτέρῳ τοιούτῳ,
i.e. they make a noise with their gills or something
of the kind.[2]

No other explanation of this fancy has ever been
given: but such a tradition cannot be founded on
nothing at all, and I believe that it arose from the
gurgling sound often made by a number of trout
freely rising together. For clearly trout could never
sing with their heads under water: and other
special reasons support this opinion. First, those
Arcadian rivers were, and are now, noted for their
abundance of trout: and next, the sound was heard
most at sunset, when after a hot day the fish would
rise, and in their swirl as well as with their gills would
make that hollow musical sound, which is as much
loved by the angler as the song of a thrush.

But it is sad to think that these waters nowadays
are netted and blasted with dynamite, not only to
provide table fish for the modern Greek, but to
furnish a large export trade.

Next as regards AElian's fly called the horsetail.
There is no doubt at all that it was a large fly: its
size is given as comparable to that of the *anthedon,*
which was some kind of wild bee, and it is quite
impossible that Mr. Lambert's rendering of *midge*
can be right. How could a midge have a colour
modelled[3] on that of the wasp, and how could it
hum like a bee ? The fly was no doubt one of the
syrphidae, which are rather smaller than hive-bee or
wasp, but have dark bodies with yellow rings upon
them. The wings are gauze-like and transparent,

---

[1] N.H. IV. 9.   [2] De An. II. 8. 15.

[3] ἀπεμάξετο is the word, and it denotes modelling, not imitating.

and it is easy to imagine that they would not stand
handling, and that the body of the fly too would
crumple on the hook. Yet the artificial fly does not
seem to have corresponded very clearly with the
natural. The cock's feather may have been a fairly
good imitation of the wings: but the body of red wool
comes nowhere near the colour of a wasp, on which
it is supposed to be modelled. AElian had not himself
seen this fly, and the likelihood is that he was not
fully acquainted with all the materials used in trying
the artificial one. There is, however, no doubt that
it was a taking pattern: for the fish rose madly to it,
as they did to the natural fly. The trout of the
Astraeus was a free-rising, sporting fish, and went for
the fly " like a bulldog," to use an analogy more
familiar now than that of a wolf or eagle: and when
Mr. Lambert speaks of him as *opening his mouth
gently* to seize his prey, he misses a good point in the
original.

One would like to know how far casting came
within the angler's tactics. A six-foot rod with
two yards of line would give little scope for that art,
though the fly may have been thrown upstream over
a rock or a ripple here and there: or it may have been
floated down in places where bush or bank con-
cealed the fisherman. The Greek word καθιᾶσι
rather suggests letting down the fly than casting;
and it may be that the Macedonian angler[1] filled his
basket by dapping.

In any case it is tolerably certain that, for sport in
that particular river with its peculiar breed of flies,
the angler must have kept his fly *floating*: the whole
context shows that the sunken fly would have been
rejected. In fact we have here the first authentic
instance of dry-fly fishing.

---

[1] It is just worth notice, that the angler, though fishing in fresh
water, is called ἁλιεύς, and his knowledge of the art is called
ὁροθηρική.

Mr. Radcliffe, however, has no difficulty in showing that fly-fishing in itself, as contrasted with bait-
fishing, was nothing very novel, although the above
account as it reaches us is more detailed than any
other in Greek or Latin literature. Why then does
AElian make so much of it ? The question may be
an idle one: for Aelian was a very gossipy writer,
and every sort of anecdote found a welcome in his
commonplace book, too often regardless of weight
or value. But it is not hard to believe that the very
fact of a floating fly, dressed in imitation of the local
fly, being the only killer on the Astraeus, seemed to
him to demand a special record.

He was quite familiar with the use of artificial
baits in general, and in another passage[1]—that in
which he says that rod-and-line fishing is the most
skilful form of angling and the one most becoming
to gentlefolk—he gives a list of the various kinds of
tackle required for fishing in general, *i.e.* for sea-
fishing as well as river. For fresh water, he
says, "one must have horse-hair of black, white,
chestnut, and light grey colour: of dyed colours
light blue and purple are preferred: and all others
are said to be worthless. Wild boar's bristles are
also used and rosin: plenty of bronze and lead:
string and feathers, black, white, and variegated.
Anglers also require crimson and purple wools, and
corks, and stakes:[2] iron (perhaps iron wire), reeds of
a good growth, rushes dry and soaked, a well-trimmed
light rod, and a rod of cornel wood: also the horns
and hide of a goat. These are for the different kinds
of fishing, which I have spoken about."

Various, indeed, are his materials, and jumbled
together without order. He goes far beyond the
needs of the sportsman-angler, whom he was prais-

[1] N.H. XII. 43.
[2] ξύλοις. The meaning is quite uncertain: but probably the
word refers to stake-nets, an interpretation which the close connexion with corks tends to confirm.

ing: for the reeds and rushes and withys (which he had mentioned just before) could only be of service to the weel-poacher, whom he had condemned, while the corks and nets point rather to sea-fishing, to which department the goat's horns and hide most certainly belong. For this equipment was used by fishermen who believed that certain fish called sargues were very much in love with goats, and whenever a herd of goats was taken down to the sea for a bathe, the sargues heard their bleating and rushed together in tumultuous joy, leaping up on the shelving rocks and crowding round the herd with gambols and tokens of delight. A fisherman, marking a sunny shallow such as the sargues frequent, arrays himself with the goatskin and horns, groundbaits the place with cakes made of barley meal and goat's flesh, and then, when the fish are thoroughly beguiled, he wields a rude rod and lands a fine catch of fish.[1]

Belief in this very silly and not very savoury story most probably made AElian include the goat equipment in his catalogue of the angler's requirements, though it is just possible that he entered that item by way of a joke. Other items, however, must relate to fly-fishing. The horse-hair served in place of the modern gut casts, between hook and line, and the four colours—black, white, reddish, and grey —were adapted for different rivers or different states of the water. The bronze is for hooks, the lead for sinkers: but the thread, the red and purple wools, and the feathers of different colours were undoubtedly meant for fly-tying. Not only, then, was AElian fully acquainted with the artificial fly as fished on the Astraeus, but he regarded it as part of an ordinary angler's outfit.

Though he was a great traveller in Greece, and a good enough Greek scholar to prefer writing in

[1] Oppian, Hal. IV. 308-373. Lines 593-615 recount the capture of sargues by divers, who use only the hand.

Greek, AElian was really a Roman of Praeneste, so that he derived his earliest impressions of angling and other sports from Italy. It is not surprising, therefore, that he knew something of fly-fishing in his native country before he wrote about it on the Astraeus, and that consequently he did not regard the Macedonian practice as a startling innovation. The evidence for this prior knowledge is furnished in part by himself, in part by Martial. AElian's own testimony is as follows:

" In the river Tecinus[1] in the north of Italy there is found a fish called thymalus (thyme-fish), about eighteen inches long, and in appearance something between a basse and a grey mullet. When taken, it has a scent which is very remarkable: for there is no whiff of that fishy smell common in all other cases, but you would think you were handling a bunch of freshly gathered thyme[2]—indeed the scent is delicious—and anyone would believe that the creature was stuffed full of the herb which is the favourite food of bees and which gives the fish its name. The easiest way of taking this grayling is by netting: it cannot be caught with a baited hook, either with pig's fat or winged ant, shell fish, or fish gut, or snail's tendon,[3] the only successful bait being the mosquito—that detestable animal which is man's enemy by day and night alike by reason of its sting and its buzzing, but which is the only delight for the grayling, and does capture him."[4]

I have translated this passage in full because of its

---

[1] Not given in the usual geographies, but clearly the Ticino.

[2] The text gives $\theta\acute{\upsilon}\mu\alpha\lambda o\nu$, but either $\theta\acute{\upsilon}\mu\alpha\lambda o\nu$ there is another form of $\theta\acute{\upsilon}\mu o\nu$ or the text is corrupt and $\theta\acute{\upsilon}\mu o\nu$ should be written. To translate as if the fish were intended is to create absurdity.

[3] By *tendon* must be meant the thick muscular structure, or " foot," on which the snail crawls.

[4] AElian, N.H. XXIV. 22. The word for this insect is $\kappa\acute{\omega}\nu\omega\psi$, which apparently means a gnat or mosquito: the two differ only in name. $\Sigma\acute{\epsilon}\rho\phi o\varsigma$ cannot mean a gnat, and is a flying ant, as I have recorded it.

importance. Mr. Radcliffe deals with it,[1] and shows
how very difficult it is to imagine in those times a
hook small enough to impale a mosquito; but he
does not draw what seems to me the clear and necessary conclusion. He speaks as if only the natural
fly were in question, and he leaves the puzzle without
a solution. But surely AElian may have in mind,
here as in the Astraeus, an artificial fly. That the
Ticino grayling was taken with a fly is past question:
it is past question too that AElian dwells on the im-
possibility of fixing the big fly of the Astraeus on a
hook without so spoiling it that no fish would look
at it: how then could so small a fly as a mosquito
be so mounted on a hook—even if a diminutive hook
were then known—as to keep its natural form and
semblance on the water and so prove a successful
lure for the grayling? Such a feat of skill is hardly
to be imagined as possible. But, if not, it follows
that the fly which proved the only killing bait on the
Ticino was an artificial fly, dressed perhaps on a
somewhat larger scale than the natural model, but
still a work of art, deftly made with the help of
feathers, wool, and thread, which AElian records as
part of an angler's ordinary outfit.

It seems, then, fair to me to claim this as another
instance of the practice of fishing with artificial flies
in the late first or the second century of our era.
That Martial gives incidentally a notice of fly-fishing
even before AElian is well known, though there is
nothing at all in his brief record to show that he had
any idea of hand-made flies being used by anglers.
The poet is speaking of what he might aptly have
called "fishing presents," *i.e.* trifling presents
made by toadies to rich men in hope of securing a
large return, and his words are as follows:

> Odi dolosas munerum et malas artes.
> Imitantur hamos dona: namque quis nescit
> Avidum vorata decipi scarum musca ?[2]

[1] Page 193.   [2] Ep. V. 18.

i.e. " I hate these cunning tricks of making gifts, when
presents are baited hooks.   All know how the greedy
wrasse swallows the fly and is fooled."

How near do these metaphors come to modern
phrases like fishing for compliments, angling for
favours, throwing a fly over a man, and so forth.
A question, however, has been raised whether a fly
is mentioned at all in the passage cited, it being
suggested by Brodaeus and other learned commen-
tators that *musco* ought to be read instead of *musca*,
so that in fact the bait which Martial was thinking
of was not a fly at all but a piece of *moss* !   Mr. Radcliffe[1] has well exposed the absurdity of this pedantic
emendation, which rests on no manuscript authority
whatever, but is prompted by a passage in Athenaeus,
who alleges, copying Aristotle, that the wrasse feeds
on seaweed and is caught by seaweed.   Many strange
stories are told about the wrasse.   It is never caught
at night by fishermen—therefore it sleeps: it moves
its gills a good deal—therefore it ruminates or chews
the cud: it sings with a liquid note—which is even
more marvellous than the song of the trout in
Arcadia: and finally it is the only fish which feeds
on herbs or grasses.   Setting these supposed endow-
ments of the scarus together in this manner, one
may judge how much credence is to be given to any
one of them, such as the seaweed habit for instance.
But Mr. Radcliffe has argued the matter at so great
a length and with so much reason, logic, and knowledge, that his conclusion in favour of the original
reading *musca* seems to me firmly established.

Granted, then, that we have here another instance
of fishing with a fly, one may also I think agree
with his opinion that the fly must have been artificial.
As he says, the fact that the wrasse is a sea fish
makes it less probable that the natural fly could have
been kept on the hook, nor could the rod have been

---

[1] Pages 152-159.

ROMAN SEA-SIDE VILLA AND FISHING SCENE.
From a Pompeian painting.

To face page 173.

wielded with much confidence. But, natural or artificial, the fly was known to Martial and to all his readers as a decoy for fish in common and familiar use, and it is he who gives the first record of its employment.

For Martial was born fifty years before AElian, and Mr. Radcliffe must forgive me if I say the difference in time between the two is not two centuries but half a century.[1] But if, as is now known, fly-fishing was practised in the first century of our era, why, it will be asked, are we dependent for our knowledge of the fact on three or four casual mentions in classical authors, and why do we not find a body of direct evidence placing the matter beyond all need of argument ? The question is not altogether an easy one to answer. There is no definite essay on fishing in Latin except Ovid's Halieutica, of which only a fragment remains, and which was probably written in his exile far from Rome. So far as it goes, it deals rather with fish than with fishing, and tells us nothing new about the art. One point, however, may be worth making. Though Martial was a native of Spain, he was living at Rome when he wrote the epigram in question, and one is bound to assume that he was thinking of fishing near Rome and used language clearly understood by his friend or patron, Quintianus: indeed he speaks of fly-fishing as a matter of common knowledge in so many words.

But why sea-fishing ? It may be remarked that although one of the commonest subjects in the many wall paintings of Pompeii is angling, in almost every instance it is angling by the sea or in a fresh-water lake. There is no record, I believe, of a river scene

[1] On p. 152 he says that the reference in Martial " certainly antedates by some two centuries the passage from AElian " (XV. 1). Martial lived roughly from about A.D. 30 to A.D. 104, AElian A.D. 80 to A.D. 140: indeed, just before Martial went back to Spain to die he may have known AElian as a young student in Rome.

or a tumbling trout stream: and sea-fishing was a
much more familiar business than river-fishing in
the south of Italy. Besides, there is another clear
case of the artificial fly being used in sea-fishing,
and this again is given by AElian[1] in some detail.

He is telling of a " rather unusual way of fishing
for pelamyds " (which were wrongly identified by
Pliny[2] and others as young tunnies). Ten young
fellows, he says, in the very flower of their age,[3]
embark on a boat which must be very light and
therefore very fast, and, after ranging themselves
on either side and eating a very hearty meal, they
take to the oars and pull in one direction or another,
more or less at random. One man seated at the
stern lets out a couple of lines, one at either side the
boat, and from each of these lines others are sus-
pended, all fitted with hooks. Every hook carries
*a bait made of Laconian purple wound about with
white wool, and every hook has also a sea-mew's
feather attached,* so that it flutters gently as the water
heaves against it. The pelamyds rise keenly at the
sight, and as soon as the first and greediest has the
hook well in his mouth, the others sail up, and the
hooks whirl about, every one buried in a fish.
Thereupon the men stop rowing, ship their oars,
and stand up to haul in the lines, which show great
sport and are heavily laden with fish.

The foregoing paragraph is AElian's own story in
his own words. It might have come in an earlier
chapter in this book which dealt with sea-fishing;
but it has been reserved for a place here in connexion
with the question of artificial baits: for it proves
undeniably that Martial's fly-fishing for the wrasse
was not a solitary instance, and that an artificial
fly was used in pelamyd fishing. The dressing of this

---

[1] N.H. XV. 10.   [2] N.H. IX. 13.
[3] Here again is a contradiction of the absurd fiction that the
fisherman was an aged and miserable toiler.

fly is interesting. One cannot imagine the hook to have been a small one, but the shank was first covered with Laconian purple, though whether this was a real purple or crimson is not certain. Then came white wool, which obviously cannot have overlaid the purple so as to cover it, else there would be no sense in having a purple foundation. It follows that the white wool was in threads or bands wound about the purple, making a very pretty pattern for the body. Last there was the sea-mew's feather, which was designed to float the fly on the surface, as the boat rowed swiftly and the lines trailed at some distance in the water. Nothing is said about the size of the feather; but beyond all doubt it was a small feather; because if anything like a large one, such as a wing feather, had been tied on to the hook, it would have been totally impossible for the pelamyds to have swallowed the bait in the easy and voracious manner recorded in the story. In fine, it is shown true, as a mere matter of logic, that the young fishers in this particular form of sport used artificial flies having a passable resemblance to modern salmon-flies.

It is also true that their method of fishing with lines trailing behind the boat and carrying a large number of flies was something between harling for salmon and working a poacher's otter, as it is called, *i.e.* trailing a piece of wood to which short lines are attached, well baited with flies. The fact that the pelamyd frequented river estuaries, where salt and fresh water meet,[1] may or may not be significant as prompting the thought that such flies may easily have been used also in river-fishing: for AElian gives no hint of the locality which he had in mind, though it may be assumed that it was somewhere off the Italian coast.

However that may be, we have now four definite

---

[1] Oppian, Hal. I. 113-118.

records of fly-fishing—one due to Martial and three
to AElian, two in fresh water and two in salt water.
Geographically, as far as one can judge, two cases
are concerned with sea - fishing off the coast of
southern Italy, one with an inland river, the Ticino,
in north Italy, and one with a river in Macedonia.
The very variety of the different conditions, together
with the remoteness of the places, one from another,
suggests forcibly that the art of fly-fishing was far
more widely known and practised than would appear
from what one must still call its scanty literary
record.   It has been shown that in the case of hunting, mention of essential factors is sometimes quite
casually omitted as taken for granted: and so here
the use of the fly in the first and second centuries of
our era was treated as matter of common knowledge,
and direct mention of it is more or less accidental.
How many little details of Greek and Roman life
have been utterly lost for the same reason ? Not
for want of a bard so much, as because he, the bard,
has said to himself like Martial *quis nescit*? *i.e.*
everybody knows all about it, and therefore it is
waste of time to treat of it in this history.

So far, however, it may be claimed that something very like a salmon-fly has been discovered:
and what of salmon ? The name certainly was
known as early as the first century in Latin, but
the salmon was not a Mediterranean fish, it has
no name in Greek, and it seems to have been known
to the Romans only after the conquest of Gaul.
Pliny is the first to mention it,[1] and his only remark
is that in Aquitania the river salmon is more highly
esteemed for the table than any sea-fish whatsoever.
Three hundred years later the poet, Ausonius, who
was a native of Aquitania, speaks of trout, salmon,
and salmon-trout or sea-trout, in the Moselle. He
calls the trout *salar* and describes it as speckled with

[1] N.H. IX. 32.

red spots:[1] a few lines lower of the *fario* he remarks
that it comes in between salmon and trout, is both
and neither, no longer a trout and not yet a salmon
—words which point clearly to salmon-trout, but
which do not quite remove all doubt whether the
poet considered that fish as a separate species.[2]
We have thus both salmon and salmon-fly, but no
proof unfortunately of their coming together. It
is a reasonable surmise that before the fourth
century the fly must have been known to anglers
in the salmon rivers of the West. Mr. Radcliffe
alleges[3] that the salmon is sometimes represented
pictorially, and refers to plate 8 in the Roman
Antiquities at Lydney Park by C. W. King (Lond.
1879) for a coloured mosaic, which was dedicated
by Flavius Senilis, commanding the Roman fleet on
the Severn, and which shows several salmon: and
plate 13.3 displays a diadem of beaten bronze repre-
senting " a fisherman in a pointed cap in the act
of hooking with undoubtedly a *tight* line a fine
salmon." Here at any rate we have in Britain an
example of salmon-fishing with rod and line—as
opposed to netting—in Roman times, and if anyone
chooses to believe that an artificial fly also was used,
who shall gainsay it ? Be that as it may, it brings
the Romans a little nearer to us today to think of
them as fully appreciating the flavour of salmon
from the Severn or the Wye, just as they enjoyed
the flavour of the oysters from the beds at Richborough.[4] Even, however, if rod and fly be granted,
it is not easy to overcome the remaining difficulty.

[1] Mos. X. 88: purpureis stellatus tergora guttis. In l. 97 he
speaks of the salmon as poeniceo rutilantem viscere, *i.e.* with pink
flesh, so that to him poeniceus denoted a lighter red.

[2] Id. ib. 128-130. [3] Page 195, n. 1.

[4] Juvenal, IV. 141, speaks of a *gourmet* in Rome telling at the
first taste whether his oysters came from Richborough or from
beds nearer home. Kentish oysters, then, were exported to Italy,
but of course English salmon was unknown, and could only be
eaten in England.

For it is quite certain that a salmon, though of moderate size, could not have been played and held successfully with a short line; in other words running tackle of some sort was necessary. Now there is no record even of a top ring on a Roman rod. It may have been just one of those things omitted by writers as not worth mention: yet the ring would not have answered alone, *i.e.* without a long line, which must have been coiled in some fashion, whether on the bank of the river or the thwart of a boat: and he would have been a monstrous skilful angler who with no better equipment could keep his line out of tangle and land his salmon.

CHAPTER XI

FOWLING

Plato's Knowledge of Sport—His Views on Fowling—Xenophon
and Cyrus—Methods of Taking Birds—Netting Quail—
Fowling by Music—Decoy Birds—Partridges—Birdlime—
Fowling Rod—Proof that it was Jointed and Tapered—Not
first mentioned by Martial—Goes back to Third Century
B.C.—Nooses, Springes, Snares, Slings—Painted Wooden
Decoy Ducks—Hawking—Bow and Arrow—Shooting Flying.

IT may seem a paradox, but it is true, that Plato
was something of an all-round sportsman—in
sympathy if not in practice. I have already shown
how warmly he praises and how keenly he en-
courages hunting. As a philosopher and as a patriot
he had to weigh every form of sport in order to
ascertain its value in the process of forming mind
and character and of shaping men for the service of
the State. Hence he deprecates—mildly deprecates
—fishing as not productive of those qualities, bodily
and intellectual, which in his theory most needed
development: but so far from saying that it is an
unworthy pursuit, he expressly acknowledges that it
may have an overpowering charm. Plutarch in a
dialogue[1] makes one of the speakers allude to Plato's
opinions on field sports and then proceed to con-
demn angling roundly, for many reasons, but chiefly
because it is " unworthy of a gentleman "—which
Plato never said. But this condemnation of angling
in Plutarch is merely dramatic—a piece of special
pleading in a discussion—and must not be read as
Plutarch's own opinion or that of Plato.

On the other hand Plato does say that fowling is

[1] De Soll. An. IX.

not altogether worthy of a gentleman: but so far is he from denouncing fowling *as a sport*, that here again he admits that it possesses its own enchantment. For he speaks of the *passion* for fowling, and in the same breath with which he calls it unworthy he terms it also bewitching.[1] He was in fact standing on the lofty heights of his theory, and his view there was detached from the world of sport. His ideal statute, however, or canon allows fowling in wild open country or on the mountains without let or hindrance, but prohibits it strongly on cultivated land or sacred ground, whence it is a public duty to warn off any fowler.

How strong a dominion this witching power of the sport held over young fellows of good family is proved in the case of Cyrus, whose training for war and the serious business of life was largely founded on lessons derived from the sports to which he was devoted. " You often used," says Xenophon, " to get up in the dark in the hardest winter weather, and set your nets or traps before the birds were stirring, so that the place you chose should seem entirely undisturbed: and your trained birds worked with you against their mates, while you lay in ambush, seeing without being seen, and practised catching the birds before they could take wing."[2]

In this particular instance it is clear that Cyrus was fowling by decoys: but even so, the sport that could pull him out of bed in the depth of winter and plant him before dawn in a frozen forest to watch for the birds' awakening was one with magic enough to charm the mind of the sportsman. Plato was right. He knew that fowling had a real fascination for his young pupils, but that it was not a discipline of sterling value. Few of them would go

[1] Legg. VII. *sub fin.* The words are μηδ᾽ αὖ πτηνῶν θήρας αἵμυλος ἔρως οὐ σφόδρα ἐλευθέριος ἐπέλθοι τινὶ νέων.

[2] Xen. Cyr. I. 6. 39. This illustration is used in connexion with military ambush.

bird-hunting, as he calls it, with ἄλγεα πάσχειν
for their maxim, or with the resolute self-denial
shown by the stripling Cyrus. It was altogether
too soft a pastime. As Oppian said much later,[1] the
fowler's work is delightful: he wants no weapons
of war, but carries net, and bird-lime, and rods,
while he roams the forest with a hawk for his companion. The same thought is found in the Ixeutica: the fowler has no perils to face: he need not
climb up to mountain tops or down into ravines:
he has only to roam the plains and brakes and
meadows, listening to the sweet notes of song-birds.

In Oppian's list two methods of taking birds are
omitted—by shooting and by decoys: but it does not
follow that six instruments, viz. net, rod, bird-lime,
hawk, decoy, and arrow, denoted separate branches
of the sport, inasmuch as two or more of those accessories of the chase were often used in combination.
The mere netting or trapping of birds was an art of
primitive antiquity on which few words are needed.
When Odysseus, as he is about to hang the treacher-
ous handmaids of Penelope, slings his ropes from
the dome of the hall, he compares them to a net
set in a bush into which birds tumble at roosting-
time.[2] The meaning of the simile is that the nooses
dangling from the pillar or beam above resembled
the meshes of a net into which thrushes or doves
flying were caught by the throat and so slain.

But nets were often set in the open, as well as in
a bush or thicket, especially in the seasons for the
migration of quail overseas. Callimachus[3] says that
in Egypt the priests of Zeus offered up prayers for
a north wind to bring a good flight of quail into the
nets on the coast: and precisely the same method
of planting on the shore nets into which the birds
plunge, weary with their long travel, is employed

---

[1] Cyn. I. 62.   [2] Od. XXII. 465-473.
[3] In Oxyrhynchus Papyri, Vol. VII.

by the Beduin and others today. This custom of fowling is in fact almost as immemorial, though not so mysterious, as the law of nature which governs the flight of the quail from far south in Africa across the Mediterranean, across Europe as far as England, and even across St. George's Channel. Pliny has some curious remarks on quail.[1] They fly in masses so dense, he says, that at night they often strike the sails of vessels at sea with such force as to capsize and sink them; further that they are banned from the table for two reasons—because their favourite food is a poison berry, and because they alone of all the brute creation are subject to epilepsy! One wonders where and how this local superstition arose, and can hardly think that it prevailed in Rome in Pliny's time. Now at any rate the poor little quail, ship-destroying, man-destroying,[2] epileptic though he were, has recovered his character the world over, and few are the tables at which he is not warmly welcomed today.

But there was another way of taking doves by netting, and one may call it musical fowling. It required the most accomplished craftsmen of the sport, and was managed successfully as follows. A small company take their stand in a wood where they dance and sing most musically. The doves, charmed by the carol and the movement of the dance, draw nearer: whereupon the company retires with slow and noiseless steps to a place where an ambush of netting is spread, and by dance and song the birds are taken captive.[3] This is a curious story, and one may pause a moment to remark how strongly the Greeks believed in the power of music, even as an aid in the realm of sport. Surely the Orphic tradition lingered still in all the wild life of Hellas.

[1] N.H. X. 32.
[2] Like Helen—ἐλέναυς ἐλάνδρος: Aesch. Ag. 689.
[3] AElian, N.H. I. 39.

GAME BIRDS, HARE, EELS, MUSHROOMS, IN
ROMAN LARDER.

From a Pompeian painting.

To face page 182.

Here is musical fowling: above I have spoken of musical hunting and of singing fish: that musical fishing was practised is shown by examples from different authors cited by Mr. Radcliffe.[1] The same love of music is shown in AElian's account of the nightingale: which he calls the clearest and sweetest of singers, warbling in lonely places notes of purest harmony.[2] Then referring to the saying that the nightingale's flesh is a remedy for somnolence, he adds: Sinners are they and unspeakable blockheads, who eat of such a dish; and sinful is the gain of driving sleep away—sleep, which, as Homer says, is king of gods and men.

The singing decoy bird was in as common use with the fowlers of Greece and Rome as it is with the bird-catchers of the New Forest today. Oppian, for example, speaks of a man hiding in thick bushes while the decoy, the familiar companion of his sport, pipes her song, and lures birds of her own feather to the trap snare.[3] The trap in vogue, too, was the same with its bait of corn outside the cage, plenty of corn within, the door propped up by a peg, to which a long string was attached and held by the fowler in ambush.

At a later date Paulinus Nolanus (fourth century), in a letter to a friend with a present of fig-eaters, says they were caught on limed twigs by a fowler who lay hidden in bracken imitating the call of birds, and who when he got home ranged his game in order on the board—a point not before mentioned. Whether whistles were used as bird-calls in classic times is uncertain, though Demetrius of Constantinople gives instructions for making such a call of cherry wood.

[1] Page 242 and n. 2.
[2] N.H. I. 43.
[3] Hal. IV. 120-126. Here differing from Prof. Mair I render ηθάδα by *familiar*, not *tame*. Oppian's account of the trap with bait is in Hal. II. 99-104.

Tame partridges were often used as decoys, and in pairing time, according to Pliny,[1] the fowler with a hen partridge captured cock birds one after another. Even a sitting bird, if she spies a male making for the hen decoy, will often rush forward so mad with jealousy that she will settle on the head of the trapper. If, however, he comes near the nest when the young are hatched out, she runs to his feet pretending to be clumsy or lame, then after a short flight tumbles feigning a broken wing or leg, and so draws him well away from the nest. This clever piece of acting by the partridge has not changed in the last two thousand years.

One other mode of bird-catching, which also has some counterpart in modern times, requires notice as involving a matter of interest to anglers. A very effectual bird-lime was made from mistletoe berries, or from oak-sap.[2] It was used in two ways principally. In the first a number of short stakes were set in the ground, their tops heavily smeared with bird-lime, and tempting food was scattered about, while the hunter lay in close concealment, watching and sometimes calling, imitating the note of the quarry.[3] Birds coming to feed naturally perched on the stakes, and their feet were held fast till the hunter released and captured them. In the other method the lime was spread on the point of a rod carried by the fowler, who moved with extreme caution to spy out a bird sitting on a tree or bush. When the bird was found, he stealthily lifted the rod, raising the point by imperceptible degrees to within striking distance, and then by a sudden thrust pushed it against the bird, whose feathers were

---

[1] N.H. X. 51.

[2] Called δρυὸς ἰκμὰς in Anth. P. VI. 109, by Antipater (first century B.C.), and δρυὸς ἰδρὼς is quoted from Ion by Athenaeus; it means sap from the tree, or perhaps from the bark. Ion wrote in the fifth century B.C., so that the practice was very ancient.

[3] Martial, Ep. XIV. 218.

hopelessly entangled. A small bird was probably
pulled down at once: a larger one, such as a wood-
pigeon, would find one of its powerful wings so
clogged that it would lose its balance and tumble to
the ground.

Here, then, we have a fowling-rod at work: the
question arises, how did it differ from the fishing-rod?
Not in name: for the terms ῥάβδος or δόναξ in Greek,
arundo or *calamus* in Latin, remain the same: nor is
there any reason to suppose that any different material
was used for the fowling-rod: but can the resemblance
be carried further? Clearly a rod with a slender top,
while often useful and often used for fishing, would
seldom serve the fowler's purpose, as it would not
hold enough bird-lime and would not have resistance
enough for any but the very smallest birds. The
fowler wanted therefore a stiff and not a whippy
rod. But as the angler required rods of different
length—from the six-foot rod used for trout on the
Astraeus to one of at least twelve feet, used for sea-
fishing—so the fowler, having to deal with birds
perching on boughs at varying heights, needed to
vary the length of his weapon.[1] In one particular
kind of his hunting he certainly carried what may be
called a rod of stock pattern. This is established in
the passage from Ion which I referred to in a note
on a preceding page. Ion there uses the expression
θαμνομήκης ῥάβδος, which Liddell and Scott render
(but quite wrongly) as a rod *cut from a bush*. Surely
the right meaning is *of the measure of the bush*,[2]
i.e. bush-high, and the poet is thinking of a fowler
in a copse or brake, where the bushes are perhaps
eight feet to ten feet high, and where accordingly
a short rod, and no other, would serve his purpose.

Where, however, the search lay not among thick

---

[1] The *arundo donax* would furnish a serviceable rod of any
length required up to at least 20 feet.

[2] The analogy of οὐρανομήκης is decisive.

bush, but among forest trees, a longer rod would be
required to reach the quarry. But it is obvious that
the fowler out for a day's sport must often be prepared
for either event, and so must be equipped with two
rods—short and long: nor is it less clear that the
task of working his way through thicket or forest
so equipped would be very troublesome. Hence it
follows that what he required, if only for convenience
of travel, was a short rod *which could be lengthened
at will*, in other words a rod with joints which could
be fitted together. This theory seems borne out by
fact. Mr. Radcliffe has debated the question[1] and
on the evidence which he produces claims that the
jointed rod was known in fowling, if not in fishing,
and that the first mention of it occurs in Martial's
couplets:

> Non tantum calamis sed cantu fallitur ales,
>   Callida dum tacita crescit arundo manu:

and again:

> Aut crescente levis traheretur arundine praeda,
>   Pinguis et implicitas virga teneret aves.[2]

There is no room for doubt that the action described
by *crescit* was that of lengthening the rod upwards in
the direction of the bird. This might be done for
a short distance by merely raising the arm: but
remembering the difficulty, which I have stressed,
of carrying a long rod through tangled forest, one
may fairly argue that the rod was lengthened by the
addition of one or more joints: for if the fowler had
his rod in three or four pieces, it could easily have
been taken through the covert. Mr. Radcliffe
quotes a line from Silius Italicus in the same sense,
but one line only, which does not register the capital
importance of the passage. A man discovered
hiding in a tree-top to escape his enemies, and there

---

[1] Pages 147-151.   [2] Ep. XIV. 218 and IX. 54.

slain, is compared to a bird marked for prey by a fowler:

> Ut qui viscatos populatur arundine lucos,
> Dum nemoris celsi procera cacumina sensim
> Substructa certat tacitus contingere meta,
> Sublimem calamo sequitur surgente volucrem.[1]

The last line is the one usually quoted, but it adds nothing to the information given by the poet's contemporary, Martial. In the second line, however, a double stress is laid on the height of the bird above the ground—*perching on the topmost boughs of a lofty tree*; and in the third the fowler is quietly *building up the tapering column of his rod* to reach the bird. It is certain that a bird so far aloft could not be touched by any rod of a single piece, and that the building-up process must mean lengthening the rod by joining other pieces to it.[2]

Even if the use of *meta* here may seem a little odd, there is no doubt at all about the meaning. The word is used to denote any tapering object, and Livy employs it to denote a conical hill. Walter's Classical Dictionary defines *meta* as "an object of tapering form on a broad circular base." The note in Drakenborch's edition of Silius is very explicit: "dum viscatae harundini aliae ex aliis harundines atque illae crassiores crassioresque substruebantur, forman metae reddebant ut pyramidis," *i.e.* precisely, as joint was added to joint the rod took the form of a tapering column. Nothing

---

[1] Sil. Ital. VII. 674-7. Oppian also expresses clearly the height to which the rod must rise when he says that it walks on a path through the air (Cyn. I. 66).

[2] Mr. Radcliffe gives a cut from a lamp in the British Museum Catalogue of Lamps (pl. 24, fig. 686). It represents an animal (perhaps a cat) with a coat and hood touching a bird on a tree with limed rod and carrying spare joints in its hand—an amusing caricature. The new catalogue now labels it Fox and Crow, with a query: and the query is justified. But the evidence of this piece is really not very important.

could be plainer: but the note is wrong in suggesting
an absurdly thick and heavy butt and build for the
rod instead of a light rod with gentle taper.

Equally decisive are some lines of Valerius
Flaccus:

> Qualem populeae fidentem nexibus umbrae
> Si quis avem summi deducat ab aere rami,
> Ante manu tacita cui plurima crevit arundo:
> Illa dolis viscoque super correpta sequaci
> Implorat ramos atque irrita concitat alas.[1]

It is the same picture: a bird settled on a tree-top
and sheltered by the leaves: a fowler below unseen,
who with noiseless hand lengthens his rod by several
joints (*plurima*): the bird-lime on the top rises
higher and higher (*sequaci*), till it reaches the feathered
prey: then the bird screaming and beating its wings
in vain is pulled down and captured.

Now all these three poets—Martial, Silius Italicus,
and Valerius Flaccus—were contemporary and all
belong to the first century of our era: so that, if it
be granted that the use of a jointed rod for fowling
is proved, there is no reason for saying that the first
mention is made by Martial rather than by either
of the other two. The truth is that the use was in
common knowledge at that epoch and therefore was
not at all novel. This inference is made certain
by a poem in the Greek Anthology,[2] in which a
fisherman past work dedicates to Priapus the
weapons of his craft, and among them δόνακα
τριτάνυστον, his "thrice-extended rod," *i.e.* three-
jointed rod, a meaning not open to question. The
author of this poem, Archias, was the friend of
Lucullus, and well known also in Rome from the
oration delivered by Cicero in his defence. His
mention of the jointed rod is, therefore, at least a
hundred years prior to that of Martial and his com-

---

[1] Argon. VI. 260-264.   [2] Anth. P. VI. 192.

peers. Bianor's words of a fowler as δοννακόεντα
συνθεὶς δόλον¹ may possibly betoken the putting-
together of a rod: but as the quarry in this case was
only a cicala, not likely to be perched at any great
altitude, such a construction is open to doubt. No
such doubt, however, can attach to the evidence of
Bion, who speaks of a bird-limer as fastening all the
joints of his rod together, one above the other.²
Bion wrote somewhere about the middle of the third
century B.C.: he was thus two hundred years earlier
even than Archias, and three hundred years before
Martial, who has been wrongly credited with the
first mention of a jointed rod in classical literature.
It is also worth notice that Bion was a native of
Smyrna, Archias of Antioch, and Martial belonged
equally to Italy and Spain: so that we not only
have carried back the use of the jointed rod to about
250 B.C. (where the mention is casual and matter-
of-course) but have proved its use from one end of
the Mediterranean to the other, and its use for
fishing as well as for fowling. Further research
may perhaps yield specific evidence for an earlier
date, but even at present it is more than probable
that the rod as known in the third century B.C.
had then been in use for at least a hundred years,
and so was known to Plato.

The nature of the joint, the way in which the
pieces of the rod were fastened together, is quite
unknown, and the conjectures which have been made
are not very satisfactory.³

There is a scene in ancient Egyptian painting in
which appears a rod with the joints tied and bound

¹ Anth. P. IX. 273.
² Bion, IV. 5: τὼς καλάμως ἅμα πάντας ἐπ' ἀλλάλοισι συνάπτων.
³ Daremberg, referring to *arundo* in Petronius, Sat. 109, thinks
that the reed was used as a blow-pipe to project a bullet of clay
or lead. There is, I believe, no authority for this. It has also been
suggested that one joint of the cane rod telescoped into another.
This suggestion also has no authority and very little probability,

together with crossing strings, which would point to a sort of splicing, like that of the modern Castle-Connell rod: and it is conceivable that some such method is hinted at in the words *textis arundinibus* cited by Mr. Radcliffe[1] from Petronius. But here a fowling-rod is in question, and one cannot suppose that a fowler standing under a tree with his quarry in sight had time for such an elaborate way of jointing, nor do the words which I have given in the quotations above consist with such a method. Of course it may be that, in some cases in which the cane rod was used, canes of decreasing thickness were fitted together, each into the hollow end of the cane below: but a joint of this kind would be very frail and would break on any strain unless it were strengthened. What has to be envisaged is a rod easily and quickly put together and able to stand a fair strain without breaking: and, though this is but another guess, I see nothing unreasonable in thinking that the joints were put together and held together by metal sockets. The Greeks and the Romans, too, were accomplished metal-workers from very ancient times, and it was just as easy to forge a metal socket for a cornel rod, or even for a cane rod, as it was to forge a socket for a spear-head. Indeed the device is so very obvious that no one who has ever read Homer, or seen the surgical instruments or other scientific metal-work of later classic date, could for a moment doubt that the joining of two rods by a ferrule and socket of metal was a simple process known from remote antiquity. Moreover it is worth remark that, whenever writers like AElian or Oppian speak of bronze or other metal fittings needed by a sportsman, they always seem to assume that he himself can forge it into the required instrument.

So much for the rod—a critic may think far too

[1] Page 148.

FOWLING AND FISHING.

From an Etruscan tomb, sixth century B.C.

To face page 191.

much. But so little has been written or known
about it, and a clear understanding of its construction, nature, and uses in various forms of sport is
so important, that the critic will not easily win an
apology.

But to return from a long digression. There are
several other devices or instruments used in fowling,
such as nooses, set in the runs of game-birds or held
on poles, traps, and nets and springes and snares.
A poem by Antipater in the Greek Anthology
records a number of such engines dedicated in a
temple:

> This ragged cloud-net and this twisted snare,
> > And gins for setting with the sinew taut,
> > And stakes whose fine point in the fire was
> > > wrought,
> Springes for throttling, cages worse for wear,
> This sticky oak-glue, and this fowling-rod
> > On which the smear of bird-lime still remains:
> Snap-cord for trap nets hidden in the sod,
> > And noose to catch the neck of noisy cranes:
> To Pan, the guard of uplands perilous
> Gives Craubis, trapper, of Orchomenus.[1]

Slings also were used, but more often perhaps for
scaring birds from the cornfields than for killing
game. Much more curious are two facts about
duck-hunting. Wild-duck abounded among the
lakes and fens of Boeotia, and they are specially
mentioned by Aristophanes as brought by Boeotians
to Athens.[2] One way of hunting them was by torch-
light, when boats were probably pushed through the
reeds and the duck driven into nets: and a similar
way of hunting sea-birds by night is recorded in the

---

[1] From Amaranth and Asphodel, by A. J. Butler, 2nd edition,
p. 141: Anth. P. VI. 109.   Cf. Aristoph. Aves, 526-8.

[2] Pax, 1004.   Lake Copais would furnish most game, but there
was a good deal of marshland by the river Melas near Orchomenus
and in other parts,

Ixeutica. The other way was by wooden decoys, shaped and painted after nature, and held by a long string. Here the hunter was hidden, and slowly towing his decoy drew the duck either within range for sticks and missiles or more probably led them into a tunnel of netting, such as is well-known in England today. This conjecture is confirmed by another passage in the Ixeutica, which definitely tells of wild-geese being lured by a wooden decoy into a channel where a net suddenly closes upon them. These painted wooden decoys furnish strange examples of the nearness of the ancient to the modern world. A more original device, which has not become traditional, was the use of a painted picture as a decoy for the sea-birds called *plungers*—perhaps skua gulls. The picture showing a brightly coloured fish was painted on hard panel and anchored afloat, and the plunger diving swiftly from a height upon it broke his neck.

Pliny tells of a bird called *cheneros*, rather smaller than a goose, but does not say how it was taken: it was, however, the finest table bird in Britain. If it was the shelldrake, that bird has not maintained its reputation. Francolins, given to running rather than flying, were sometimes hunted down with dogs: while for the purple coot a man had only to dance gracefully towards his quarry, when the coot enchanted would come gaily tripping forward to meet him, and in the midst of the minuet could be comfortably knocked on the head.[1]

But it is time to say something about a more sporting form of chasing birds, viz. hawking. Unfortunately here, as in so many other cases, writers are not lavish with their information. Daremberg

[1] These curiosities may be found in Bk. III of the Ixeutica. There is an Egyptian painting in which duck-hunters in a punt among tall reeds are using throwing-sticks against the birds which they put up, and some of these throwing-sticks were curved like a boomerang and had the flight of a boomerang.

CAT AND PARTRIDGE : WILD DUCK, ETC.
From a Pompeian mosaic.

To face page 192.

goes so far as to say that hawking was unknown to the elder Pliny. This is a mistake: for Pliny distinctly mentions it,[1] though it may be that he was only quoting from Aristotle and not speaking of any practice in Italy. Yet the evidence of Martial is quite definite.[2] In an epigram of two lines he tells of a hawk, which was once chased by other birds, as trained to serve its master and prey on them. It would still be true to say that the art of hawking was far better known and earlier practised in Greece than further West. There exists in Greek an amazingly detailed and elaborate treatise called The Science of Hawking, written by one Demetrius of Constantinople: it deals with the capture of eyasses and fledgeling hawks, their breeding in captivity, their varieties, equipment and training for the field, their points of form, their accidents, ailments, and diseases, and every phase of their life and employment, in as round and ample a measure as any book on falconry in modern times. Demetrius himself, however, was a mediæval writer, physician to Michael VIII, who was Emperor from A.D. 1260-1282, and his evidence would count for little beyond the presumption of a long prior development, except for the fact that he had before him as he wrote a complete paraphrase of the Ixeutica, a poem which is wrongly assigned to Oppian. It must, nevertheless, belong to about his period, and so go back to about the second century: consequently, one may fairly regard the sport of falconry as well established by that date. Oppian himself speaks of a hawk as the familiar companion of the fowler, who is roaming the forest with rod or net or trap:[3] as if hawking were an adjunct of the other

---

[1] N.H. X. 10.
[2] Ep. XIV. 216.
[3] Cyn. I. 62. Sir John Malcolm in Sketches of Persia, Vol. I. ch. 5, gives an account of deer-hunting in which hawks and hounds work together in full intelligence.

forms of sport and were universally known. Five
centuries or so earlier Aristotle[1] says that in a district
of Thrace above Amphipolis, men go hunting in the
fens with hawks. Sticks are rattled in the reed-beds
and bushes to put up the game: when the birds are
in the air, the hawks are loosed and give chase till
they fly down again and are struck by the fowlers
and killed. The hawks always are given their
share of the spoil. It is from this that Pliny's
description of hawking is copied: but AElian tells a
somewhat different story, which represents the hawks
as driving the game to prepared netting.[2] He also
says that the Indians hunt hares and foxes without
hounds, training eagles, hawks, and crows by means
of tame hares and foxes to kill the wild ones.[3]

Aristotle names ten varieties of hawks, some of
them stooping to their quarry on the ground, some
on trees, and some in the air. The same writer
vouches for the truth that owls also were trained by
sportsmen to hunt all sorts of birds. Particulars of
this training and hunting are sadly lacking, but the
practice is said to have been derived from the fact
that owls are mobbed and worried by small birds
in the daytime. How this lesson was applied, or
how any training resulting from it could serve
against all sorts of birds, is matter of conjecture.[4]
A little light comes from the Ixeutica, which speaks
of a fowler tethering an owl to a hoop of bronze
and pulling a string from his hiding place to make
him flutter. Small birds thus coming to buffet the
owl are caught on limed twigs set round about his
perch, and are easily taken when the hunter comes
out of hiding. The same trick was played with a
sparrow-hawk: but in both cases it is decoying, and
not hawking, although the writer calls it a very
pretty sight.[5]

[1] N.H. X. 36.   [2] AEl. N.H. II. 42.   [3] Id. Ib. IV. 26.
[4] H.A. I. 1.   [5] III. 17, and III. 5.

There the matter must rest. Apparently hawking
in general, though quite familiar in classic times, did
not then become very specialised as a sport, and did
not arouse the keen enthusiasm with which falconry
was followed in the Middle Ages, both in the East
and in England,[1] and is followed now by its remaining votaries. In passing on one notes that the
varieties used in modern hawking nearly correspond
to Aristotle's in number. Falcons, or long-winged
hawks, and hawks proper, or short-winged, form the
two main divisions: in the first class are the peregrine,
the gerfalcon, and the merlin—all of ancient renown
—as well as the Barbary falcon, the snare, the lanner,
and the hobby: of the second class only the gos-
hawk and the sparrow-hawk are used for sport: and
the total is nine. But it may safely be said that there
is nothing in the Badminton book on Falconry
which surpasses the profound and minute knowledge
of the art of hawking and the care, the training, and
the equipment of the hawk, which is shown by the
Byzantine Demetrius: and it may well be that even
in Greek and Roman days the art was far more highly
developed than appears from the somewhat scanty
literature surviving. It doubtless came from the
East, where beyond all question it had flourished for
at least a thousand years before any written record
of the sport appeared in Greece or Italy.

Readers of Scott will remember the scene in
Anne of Geierstein,[2] in which Arthur Philipson,
after bending a mighty bow, shot three arrows in
quick succession at a distant mark—a pole to the
top of which a pigeon was tied by a loose cord.
The first arrow cleft the pole: the second cut the
tether: and the third pierced the pigeon as it rose in

---

[1] Shakespeare was master of every term in falconry, however
technical. Thus not a word is wrongly used by Petrucchio in his
metaphors from training of the hawk in Taming of the Shrew
(Act IV. Sc. 1 *sub fin.*).   [2] Ch. IV.

the air.   But not every reader, perhaps, knows that
this feat of archery is borrowed from Vergil, and
that Vergil borrowed it from Homer:[1] in both poets
the incident occurs in a series of athletic contests.
It shows that the ideal of quick, clean shooting was
as vivid in Homer's time as in our own, and that the
art was as much studied, however different the
weapons.

In an earlier chapter I have shown that bow and
arrow were more or less taken for granted as accessories of hunting.   One need not recall the familiar
story of the bow of Odysseus, or speculate upon its
power or range: nor need one remember in Vergil
that the war in Latium arose from a rather bad shot
at a tame deer by young Iulus.   There is no doubt
that shooting running game was an ordinary pastime,
or that the hunter took as much delight in skilful
handling of his bow and straight shooting as is taken
today by a good performer with gun or sporting
rifle.   But the really stirring question is whether
shooting flying also was habitually practised in wold
or forest: for that is a different matter from shooting
at a mark in a set competition.   The evidence is
not very conclusive.   Such an expression as pulling
a bird down (from the air) is as common in Greek
as in English: but whereas in English it would mean
pulling down a tall pheasant, for example, with the
gun, in Greek it may mean literally pulling down a
bird from a tree-top with the limed fowling-rod.
On the other hand there apparently was a separate
class of hunters called archers or shooters.   Thus
in a poem of Antipater shooting is definitely contrasted with hunting in a dedication of temple
offerings:

Arrows, a lyre, and circling mesh here set,
  By Sosis, Phile, and Polycrates—
The shooter's bow, the hunter's woven net,

[1] AEn. V. 485 *seq.*, and Hom. Il. XXIII. 850 *seq.*

The lyre from her who chanted to its keys:
May one with pride of song, one in the chase,
One with his deadly aim, take foremost place.[1]

An instance is also given of a father saving his child
by shooting through the head a serpent coiled about
him and towering over him.[2] The Cretans, as was
said above, were remarkable for their skill as archers:
and in the Anthology two little poems commemorate
the shooting of an eagle high in air.[3] Yet another
tells of a fowler with a " crow-shooting weapon,"
who used to stalk wild-geese and kill them with
long shots—sometimes on the wing, no doubt[4]: a
bird-scarer is represented as shooting at cranes in the
air[5]: and one Androclus, who was a fine shot, dedicates
his weapons to Apollo, with this inscription:

Androclus gives this bow, which aiming true
　In goodly hunting brought him many a head:
For when it bent and forth the arrow flew,
　Never it missed the mark or idly sped.
Whene'er his arrow twanged the deadly string
　It smote the prey in air or on the wold.
So, Phoebus, guard the weapon he doth bring—
　His gift set round about with bands of gold.[6]

These instances, however clear, are for the most
part rather late in date, the last cited verses being
by Paul the Silentiary and so hardly within the
classical period at all, while the lines about the eagle
were written in the first century. Still the chain
of achievements which reaches from Homer to Paul
cannot be imagined as broken at any time: nor was
shooting flying ever out of the mind of the Greek
bowman. It was perhaps a rare accomplishment
and rarely practised: for it must be considered that

---

[1] Anth. P. VI. 118. The shooter is ὀϊστευτής, the hunter
ἀγρευτής, and the chase κυνηγεσία.
[2] Id. VI. 381. 　　　　[3] Id. IX. 223 and 265.
[4] Id. VII. 546. 　　　[5] Id. VII. 172. 　　　[6] Id. VI. 75.

an arrow shot into the air from a powerful bow in rough country was lost, unless it struck the quarry full. One does not hear of Artemis shooting winged game, although her troop of maiden keepers no doubt carried plenty of ammunition. On the other hand Arcadia—that home of sport, as well as land of bliss and beauty—remembers how Heracles brought down with his bow those evil birds, the Stymphalides: and no one ever questioned that he shot them flying. The illustration shows that they were hit full in the breast while on the wing. Similarly in the Etruscan painting, which shows a hunt of ducks and other water birds, one of the men is clearly aiming at them in the air, though the weapon he is using appears to be a sling.

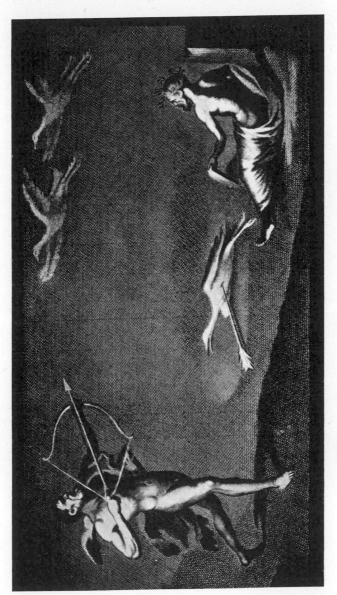

SHOOTING FLYING : HERACLES AND THE STYMPHALIDES.
From a painting at Herculaneum.

To face page 198.

CHAPTER XII

CONCLUSION

Other Sports—Plato on Chariot Racing—Cock-Fighting—Latin
Authorities on Sport generally—Sallust—Pliny the Younger
—Sport and Study—Ovid—Horace—Martial—Professor of
Angling and Moonfish—The Persian Fisherman—Greek
Sportsmen and Sporting Literature Superior to Latin—Plato
once more.

GAMES and sports, other than field-sports, are
not within the scope of this book. They have
been widely studied and are well known. Chariot-
racing no doubt demanded the utmost courage, cool-
ness, and skill, as well as knowledge of horses, and
it was no mean feat to drive four-in-hand abreast,
or even a pair, round an oval course at a furious
pace. But Sophocles, in the Electra, has left for all
time a description of such a contest which is familiar
in text or translation to most readers. One may
however remark upon it again, that while one of the
teams was Thessalian, in another team from AEtolia
the horses were all chestnuts: in another from AEnia
all white: and that as two of the drivers were Libyans,
two pairs of Libyan horses were entered. This
proves that the Libyan strain was already well
established in Greece at that period. But Plato's
opinion upon chariot-racing is certainly not so well
known as Sophocles' description. A man called
Anticeris of Cyrene, another Libyan, being vastly
proud of his riding and driving, contrived a plan
to show off before Plato in the Academy, where he
made several circuits of the road with his car at
great speed, grazing the wall all along but never
touching it, to the astonishment of all except Plato,

who gave him but cold encouragement. It is impossible, he said, for a man who has given so much thought to small and trifling affairs of this sort ever to care seriously for things of weighty importance. Having mortgaged his whole mind to those pursuits, he needs must think little of matters which really claim admiration.[1] Plato here, as in his remarks on field-sports, was thinking of the place of pastimes in education.

But is not this anecdote the original of a story told of Herbert Spencer? who, playing his customary game of mild billiards one day at the Athenæum, met with an overwhelming defeat from a new member, and remarked at the end that " a moderate skill at billiards may provide a useful recreation, but wholly abnormal dexterity of that sort can only argue a misspent youth."

Wrestling, boxing and the like manly sports must no less be left aside here, as well as other unmanly sports such as cock-fighting and partridge-fighting. It is said that after the rout of the Persians one day in every year a public festival of cock-fighting was held in the theatre at Athens, because Themistocles, when mustering the forces of the Greeks for battle, saw two cocks fighting and remarked: " These birds are suffering not for their country or the ashes of their fathers or the temples of their gods, not for glory, not for freedom, but in sheer determination not to be beaten:" and his words put fresh courage into the Athenian soldiers and sped them to victory. But in any such exhibition the moral lesson would soon fade and the mere lust of blood prevail. One may remember how even St. Augustine blazed with excitement when he went to see those contests of gladiators which he had vowed to renounce. Such

[1] AEl. V.H. II. 27, and ib. 28 for the cock-fighting story. For the latter see also Pliny, N.H. X, 24. For partridge-fighting, AEl. V.H. IV. 1. Cock-fighting is shown to the life in a Pompeian mosaic.

contests and games undeniably had their charm for
the multitude; but they are not to the purpose
here.

Little is left, then, but to put together a few
rambling notes which have not been fitted into
earlier chapters. And first something more may be
said on the question of classic sport in general.

Sallust has some remarks which are not out of
tune with Plato. A man, he says, who spends his
whole life in hunting is rather doing menial service
than taking lawful exercise: with him it is a mania,
not a pleasure. And again: " I have no great admiration for mere athletic training or muscular prowess:
but a man whose mind has sovereign control over
a body neither weakened by self-indulgence nor de-
based by wealth to sloth and luxury may take his
sport on the mountain or on the sea, and I will
admire his body rejoicing in hard work and his
limbs growing under his toil." And Sallust is right
not only in putting the things of the intellect before
sport, but in insisting that enjoyment is of the essence
of sport. So Grattius sings

" Dona cano divom, *laetas* venantibus artes,"

a line in which the famous critic Scaliger would
substitute *placidas* for *laetas*, as if the chase might be
restful, but could not be joyous ! Truly such a
scholar lived in the clouds or in some dark cavern
of learning, and he had only half the matter—
φιλομαθὴς μέν, φιλόθηρος δὲ οὔ[1]—scholar indeed,
but no sportsman. Nemesianus agrees with Grattius
in speaking of the cheery work (*hilares labores*) of
hunting. The Younger Pliny combined in a measure
the claims of study and of sport, but with all his
fine villas on Lake Como and his love of country
life he loved his books more, and was not sportsman enough to fling aside the scholar when he

[1] Plato, Rep. 535d.

took to the chase. Thus in a letter to Tacitus he says[1]:

"Laugh! and well you may. This friend of yours has captured three wild boars, and very fine ones too. *You*? quotha: Yes, I: but without wholly belying my indolent and peaceful nature. I was sitting by the nets, with neither spear nor hunting-knife at hand—only my pencil and note-book—and I was deep in thought and jotting down notes, so that I might go home with tablets full though empty-handed of game. It is not a bad way of working. Strange how action and movement of the body unsettle the mind. But the depths of a lonely forest and that deep stillness needed for hunting are most stimulating to thought. So I advise you the next time you go hunting to take not only your lunch and your flask, but your note-book as well. You will find that Minerva like Diana roams the wilds."

In another letter to Tacitus (who had recommended Pliny to vary his reading with sport) he says: "I should like to take your advice and relieve study with hunting, but boars are so scarce that it can't be done."[2] But yet again he writes: "At my villa by Como, I am hunting and working at my book—sometimes one, sometimes both, and I cannot yet say whether it is harder to take game or to write."[3] Elsewhere: "I don't wonder that you were delighted with such extraordinary sport:"[4] but what it was we are not told. He does in his Panegyric to Trajan speak of the relief which hunting and a free life on the mountains gave to the Emperor after the cares of State: and Trajan had much more of the sportsman in him than Marcus Aurelius or other Emperors. But a man like Pliny, who goes out hunting in the

---

[1] Ep. I. 6. Cf. Verg. Ecl. III. 75: Si dum tu sectaris apros, ego retia servo.

[2] Ep. IX. 10.   [3] Ep. V. 18.   [4] Ep. IX

forest and sits under a tree with a note-book in his hand, while the hunt is moving, may be a student but is sportsman no whit.

It would be strange if the same combination of sport with study in the field could be found in England in modern times, yet it has to be believed. Vlitius, who paid a visit to this country in the early seventeenth century and published some account of it,[1] says that he came to England for study, and was living in the country among a company of young fellows of good family, by whom he was prevailed upon to join a hunt for the winter. It was a thing very much against his habits, but he enjoyed it so greatly that he found the winter gone before he knew of its arrival. On off days they used to cite Xenophon, Oppian, and above all Grattius, discussing problems which they solved in practice in the field. Sometimes they carried copies of these authors with them, and note-books to enter anything worth remark: at other times they dismounted and pursued their studies in the woodland, and they found the silence required for the chase very stimulating for reflection. As Pliny says, he concludes, Minerva roams the hills even as Diana.

It is quite clear that Vlitius knew his Pliny and knew the passage for which his story makes a parallel: but it is a pity that he gives no names which would help towards identification of his friends or the place of his sojourn. Nor is there a word to show the nature of the hunting, though probably the chase was for hare or deer: for the date was at least a century before the days of fox-hunting in England.

What remains of Ovid's work on sport proves that he had imagination enough to enter into the heart of the matter, however little of it he learned in actual angling or hunting.

[1] Venatio Nov-Antiqua, Elzevir, 1644.

Horace had a poet's fancy and could paint a rural scene with soft but lively colours. Thus in the famous epode beginning " Beatus ille qui procul negotiis," he has some lines on field-sports—hunting boar with a pack of hounds and harrying them into the net, catching thrushes in a fine mesh, chasing hares, snaring cranes—and asks who, amid such pleasures, could remember the sorrows that burden his love.[1] He has heard of the hunter who is clever at bringing down a running stag with a cast of his spear or rousing a boar from the thicket:[2] and who, when his hounds have viewed a deer and are lost in the chase, or when a boar has burst through the wall of netting, stays out all day in the forest, unmindful of his young wife at home.[3] But Horace did not share in these delights: he had not the courage nor the hardihood needful for the chase. Plato fought in two battles with distinguished bravery: Horace ran away. And in one of the Epistles Horace seems rather of opinion that the final cause of hunting is food for the palate[4]—or " the pot," if colloquial idiom is preferred—though elsewhere his tone is pitched higher.

Martial apparently had some strain of sportsmanship in his blood. Thus in his verses to Maternus, his countryman at Rome, he asks him whether he would rather be catching frogs or sprats in Latium than fishing on the Spanish shore, where a mullet of less than three pounds is put back into the water as under weight ? or feeding on cockles, while in Spain even the domestics feast on oysters ? or chasing a smelly fox, while at home the nets just lifted from the sea are set for hares at once ? As I write, he adds, your angler here comes home with an empty creel, and your hunter returns mighty proud of taking a badger. Why, even the fish for the great houses

---

[1] Epod. II. 35-38. [2] Od. III. 12. 10.
[3] Od. I. 25. [4] Epist. I. 6. 56.

by the seaside in Latium comes from the market
at Rome.[1]

One must not forget that AElian, despite his writing in Greek, was a Roman, and he knew something
about angling as well as other sports. An angler
for whom he had the greatest admiration, who was
not only the first and most learned authority on the
whole science of angling, but also a most able ex-
ponent of the art, was one Demostratus,[2] a specimen
of whose learning he quotes. There is a certain
beautiful fish called the moon-fish, of no great size,
but· broad, and blue in colour: it has a heavily
crested back-fin which it can raise at pleasure: so
that when it is swimming with the fin spread it looks
like a half-moon. It is found in the waters of
Cyprus, and the description is that given by Cypriote
fishermen. Demostratus, however, says that this
fish changes with the changes of the moon—waxing
and waning with it—full-orbed at full-moon and
so forth. Moreover, if you tie it on to a tree, the
tree swells as the fish waxes and shrinks as it wanes,
and plants near it at that stage wither. It is also
of great value in well-sinking. When the diggers
have got down to water, if at new-moon a moon-
fish is thrown down the well, it ensures a perennial
spring which can never fail: whereas if the fish is
thrown in during the last quarter of the moon, the
water disappears.

It is amusing to contrast the plain tale of the local
fishermen with the embellishments of the learned
professor of angling. Alciphron in one of his
letters[3] speaks of a fisherman as a man who honestly
reveres truth and could by no possibility slip into
a falsehood. The simple seaman could not be un-

[1] Ep. X. 37, already quoted. This is the first mention of
badger-hunting—clearly a despised occupation.
[2] AEl. XV. 2. The country of Demostratus is not given.
[3] I. 21. My reference and text differ slightly from Mr. Radcliffe's.

truthful, even by accident, and added nothing to
what he saw, while the master of all the arts of
fishing, fired by the very name *moon-fish*, forged
a romantic fairy tale, unwitting of the ironic proverb
that truth lies at the bottom of a well. It surely
does him vast credit, and is vastly more pleasing
than any verity set out in dull, cold simplicity.
Even so let all good anglers win repute.

There is, however, another side to the matter.
Greeks and Romans alike strongly believed in invo-
cations to their deities before engaging, or while
engaged, in any form of sport. This belief stands
revealed at its best in the last chapter of Arrian's
Treatise on Hunting, where he names the various
gods presiding over the fortunes of the chase, and
dwells on the importance of winning their favour
by prayer and sacrifice. Call it religion or call it
superstition, it was faith: and faith could work
advantage in that sphere as in others. How often
has St. Hubert heard entreaties for aid in more
recent times ? And did not Mr. Jorrocks cry aloud
to Artemis when he was bogged in the forest morass ?

With this phase of mind one may contrast the
fatalism of the Oriental. Mr. Radcliffe[1] comes to
the conclusion that the hook was seldom if ever
used in Persian fishing. Sadi, however, in the
Ghulistan tells a story which seems to establish
angling with hook and line. A man fishing in the
Tigris got his hook into a big fish, which was too
heavy for him to land. " Fearing to be drawn into
the river himself, he abandoned the line and the
fish swam away with the bait in his mouth. His
companions mocked him, and he replied, ' What
could I do ? This animal escaped me because his
last hour fixed by destiny had not yet come. Fate
governs all, and the fisherman cannot overcome it
more than another, nor can he catch fish, even in
the Tigris, if fate be against him. That fish, even

[1] Page 51.

if he were dried, would not die, if it was the will
of fate to preserve its life.' "[1] With us an un-
successful angler would find but acid consolation in
such philosophy: but after all is the belief in luck,
and above all the silly cult of mascots, any better
than the Oriental creed of destiny ?

But to return to our Latin authorities. Both in
this chapter and in those foregoing the endeavour
has been to set down in fairness all the material
they furnish for constructing some sort of a model
of the Roman world of sport. Yet how strongly,
how swiftly, does the current of thought sweep us
back to the deep conviction that in their love of
sport, as in their love of art and of nature, the
Romans followed but never rivalled the Greeks.
They had not the long historic life of Hellas behind
them, nor the long historic literature of sport beginning with Homer, nor the traditions of sport which
were ancient long before Homer was born: they
had no one to compare with Xenophon, great com-
mander in war, great writer, and great sportsman,
some five centuries before the Roman Empire:
they had no artist of sporting scenes who could
rival the frescoes of Tiryns, the vase-paintings of
Athens, or the sculptures in marble or the bronzes
of Alcamenes, Myron, and Lysippus: and above
all they had not that same spirit of mystic delight
in nature and of joyous communion with nature,
which is of the essence of sport, and which breaks out
in such lines as these, written by Plato:

Be still, ye wooded cliffs and waterfalls,
    And mingled bleatings from the murmuring meads !
For Pan with sweetly ringing music calls
    Laying his lips on pipe of bounden reeds:
And round him dancing swift with glimmering feet
    Nymphs of the forest and the fountain meet.[2]

[1] The Rose Garden of Persia, by L. S. Costello, London, 1899.
[2] Anth. P. IX. 823.

Plato, whose genius as a philosopher opened new worlds to his contemporaries and is enshrined imperishably in all modern thought, studied and wrote poetry in his young days: he was also trained in all the manly exercises in vogue in Athens, and he knew enough of field sports to warrant a belief that they had their part in the formation of his own mind and character. But the spirit of the lines quoted did not finally prevail with him.

For lofty as was Plato's conception of sport, and great as was the value he set upon it in his scheme of morals and politics, it was perhaps a somewhat hard conception. Tried by his standard, much of what is called sport today would be condemned, and scathingly condemned, as spurious. But we do not find in Plato's theory of hunting, for example, any trace of that feeling of compassion for victims of the chase which distinguishes Arrian, yet was unknown to the Romans, by whom the noblest animals were butchered to make a holiday. Nevertheless that feeling lies at the heart of every true sportsman today, whatever may be said to the contrary. One other contrast may be drawn. In Plato's theory of sport the elements of strenuousness and self-discipline dominate all others. But in these unquiet days what is most valued—at least by the angler—is a certain refinement of mood in escape from the noise of the world, in the peace and restfulness of the riverside.

INDEX

ABARIS, 136
Achaean horses, 41, 42
Aconite, 113
Acropolis of Athens, 141
Admon, fish, 146
AElian, 35, 87, 113, 161, 163-171, 174, 176, 194
AEschylus, 106
Agassaean hound, 53
Agriophagi, 113
Albania (Georgia), 54
Alciphron, 131, 205
Alexander the Great, 30, 43, 54, 55, 118
Amia, fish, 144
Ananius, 117 n. 2, 118, 145
Angling, meaning of, 132
Anselm, Archbishop, 31
Anthedon, wild bee, 164-166
Anthias, fish, 125, 152, 154
Anthology, the Greek, 38, 80, 101, 107, 138 n. 2, 184 n. 2, 191, 196-197 and notes, 207
Anticeris of Cyrene, 199
Apollo, 22, 123, 194
Apostolides, 129
Aquitania, 176
Arab horses, 41
Arabia Felix, 91
Arcadia, 165-166
Arch of Constantine, 94
Archery, 34, 35, 96, 195-198
Archias, poet, 188-189
Argive horses, 41
Argus, hound, 17
Arion, 159
Aristaeus of Euboea, 110
Aristolochia poison, 151 n. 1
Aristophanes, 39, 191 and nn. 1 and 2
Aristotle, 118, 123, 133, 142, 143, 147 n. 3, 154, 165, 193, 194

Armenia, 41, 42, 95 n. 3, 98
Aroanius river, 165
Arrian, 28-31, 53, 67-75, 208
   criticism of Xenophon, 48-50
   pet hound, 50-51
Artemis, 19, 20, 22, 23, 35, 66, 72, 119, 120
Artificial fly, 164-169, 171, 172, 174, 176
Arundo Donax used for rod, 137, 185 n. 1.
Astraeus river, 163
Atalanta, 23
Athenaeus, 23 n. 1, 165
Athens, 73, 119, 131, 200, 207, 208
Augustus, emperor, 134
Aulopias, fish, 125, 152
Ausonius, 161, 176

Bacchus, story of, 109-111
Badminton on Hunting, 31, 52, 69 n. 1
   on Falconry, 195
Balloons or bladders, for fishing, 157
Bear, 97-101
Beaufort, Duke of, 31, 52
Beauty-fish, 154
Beckford, 32
Bellerophon, 43
Beroea, 164
Bianor, 189
Bion, 189
Bird-lime, 184 *seq.*
Bison, 106-108
Boar, *passim*
   hounds, 53
   hunting, 19 *seq.*
Bow and Arrow: see Archery
Branding horses, 45
   rogues, 141-143

14

PRINTED IN GREAT BRITAIN BY
BILLING AND SONS LTD., GUILDFORD AND ESHER

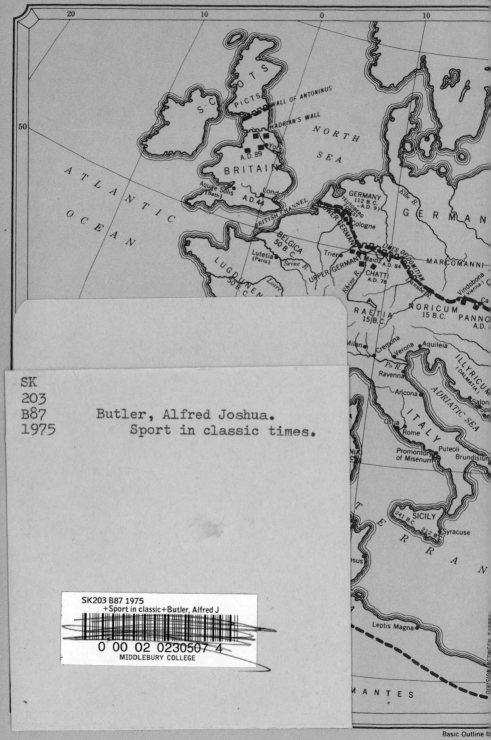

Reproduced by permission from   *The Mediterranean World In Ancient Times*